To Kill a Mockingbird,
Tender Mercies,
A N D
The Trip to Bountiful

# To Kill a Mockingbird, Tender Mercies,

AND

# The Trip to Bountiful

THREE SCREENPLAYS

BY

## Horton Foote

**GROVE PRESS**
*New York*

*Published simultaneously in Canada*
*Printed in the United States of America*

Library of Congress Cataloging-in-Publication Data

Foote, Horton.
[Plays. Selections]
To kill a mockingbird; Tender mercies; and, The trip to
Bountiful: three screenplays/by Horton Foote.
p. cm.
ISBN 0-8021-3125-5 (pbk.)
1. Motion picture plays—United States. I. Title.
II. Title: To kill a mockingbird. III. Title: Tender
mercies. IV. Title: Trip to Bountiful.
PS3511.O344A6     1989
812'.54—dc19                            88-21384

Designed by Irving Perkins Associates

Grove Press
841 Broadway
New York, NY 10003

03   10 9 8 7 6 5

*For Geraldine Page*

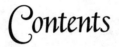

# Contents

# Foreword

I was hired to write the screenplay of *To Kill a Mockingbird* by Robert Mulligan, the director, and Alan Pakula, the producer, in 1961. I knew little about adapting or writing for the screen, having only adapted a novel, *Storm Fear*, that Cornel Wilde directed, produced, and starred in; and two Faulkner stories, *The Old Man* and *Tomorrow*, for television's "Playhouse 90." I had worked with Mulligan three times before in television. I had never worked with Pakula, who was a very young man at the time, but he'd had considerable experience in film production, and, having discussed a number of projects with him earlier, I felt very sympathetic towards his ideas about plays and films.

I worked on the screenplay in my house in Nyack, New York. Pakula would drive out to Nyack from New York City every few days and we would go over what I had written. With kindness and patience, he guided me through the screenplay until we arrived at a first draft, which we gave to Universal Pictures, our star, Gregory Peck, Harper Lee, and Robert Mulligan. After reading it, Peck asked Pakula if this was really the first draft. It was, as I remember, the fifth.

After the official first draft was finished, Pakula and I stayed on at Universal Studios to do further work on the screenplay and discuss its production with Robert Mulligan. We worked together as I had been used to working with directors and producers in the theater. I was consulted about locations, sets, costuming, and casting. I thought, "This is all very pleasant. Why are writers so unhappy out here?"

Later, I learned the answer to that all too well.

After *To Kill a Mockingbird* and a second film with Pakula and Mulligan, *Baby, the Rain Must Fall*, in 1963, my experiences in Hollywood were discouraging and often humiliating. There was a phrase, and I suppose still is, in the contracts of writers hired by studios that says in essence you are a writer for hire. They own what you have written and can edit and revise without your consent. I didn't want to be a writer for hire in Hollywood—or anywhere else—so I left and began to work again on my plays.

For me to have any chance of successfully dramatizing the work of another writer, I have to choose material that I respect and that I am in sympathy with, that deals with people and a world I understand. Whenever I've done that with Faulkner, Flannery O'Connor, or Harper Lee, I have felt a real satisfaction in the work; when I haven't, I've felt lost and confused. I felt I understood the world of Harper Lee's novel and its people. The town of the novel was not unlike the town I was born and brought up in, and the time of the novel, the depression era of the 1930s, was a period I had lived through.

After I decide to adapt a work, I read it over and over, making notes. The essential story, of course, is given you; the characters have been named and defined. Your creativity has to work within a given framework—but not in a strait jacket that reduces you to uninspired literalness. I try to absorb the author's world and to find a creative way to enter it. That can take place in many unexpected ways. With *Mockingbird*, I was very influenced in my dramatization by a review of R. P.

Blackmur's called "Scout in the Wilderness" in which he compared (very favorably) *To Kill a Mockingbird* to *Huckleberry Finn*, and the character of Scout to Huck. His review strengthened my own feelings that we should discover the evil and hypocrisy in this small southern pastoral town along with and through the eyes of the children. I was also helped by Alan Pakula's suggestion that we restructure the events of the novel which ran over several years to fit into a single year. The two approaches, one subjective and one objective, helped me to find both a style and structure for the screenplay.

It was the film version of *Tomorrow* some ten years later that revived my interest in writing for films. After its production on "Playhouse 90," Herbert Berghof staged the play in his theater at H. B. Playwrights on Bank Street, with Robert Duvall and Olga Bellin. Its limited run was a great success, and Paul Roebling and Gilbert Pearlman wanted to produce it as a film in Mississippi, again with Robert Duvall and Olga Bellin, directed by Joseph Anthony. They asked me to come to Mississippi, attend all rehearsals, and be on the set during the filming. Later in New York I was invited to participate in the editing. I had never been on a set during filming or in the editing room before, and I learned a great deal. All of my earlier films, even *To Kill a Mockingbird*, had been made on a studio back lot, and in those days the writer was sent home once filming began and, to my knowledge, was never invited into the editing room.

Editing is a very subjective process. Usually, there are a number of takes on a given scene. Many elements can influence the selection of one particular take over another: the acting, the camera angles, the look of the scene, the intended rhythm. And I learned how crucial to the final film each of these minute and seemingly endless choices are. I try to be in the editing room now as much as possible, both to learn and to express my point of view.

After the release of *Tomorrow* in 1972, I returned to writing plays. In order to help finance this, my agent, Lucy Kroll, suggested I write an original screenplay. She said if I would just submit a paragraph or two of what it was to be about, she would find a producer and a studio to give me an advance. I won't go into all the complications and hazards of such arrangements, but I ended up writing the screenplay of *Tender Mercies* with no studio assistance whatsoever.

I began *Tender Mercies* in 1979 by making notes for a screenplay about five young country-western musicians who want to become full-time professionals, but a producer who knew of the story suggested that I needed an older man as a contrast to the young men. I began to think about this older man and who he could be to fit into this world of country music. I called him Mac Sledge and I decided to make him a once-famous performer.

When you work on material of your own, you go into an uncharted world. Everything has to be found—story, character, style. At that time, I had never known any famous country-western singers, but I had known famous actors and actresses whose careers had been ruined because of drunkenness, and some who'd overcome alcoholism. I also knew about fame and loss of fame, ambition and loss of ambition. All my life I had known nonsinging Mac Sledges—pained, bewildered, inarticulate—good men really, at least with a desire to be good, whose lives were in a shambles, totally out of control.

I became obsessed with Mac Sledge and *Tender Mercies*. I put all my other writing aside and worked on it constantly. When I finished it, I took it to New York and read it to Robert Duvall, who agreed to play the part. We tried in every way to produce it ourselves, but could not get it financed.

Philip and Mary Ann Hobel came to H. B. Playwrights in 1979 to see a production of *1918* and asked to produce that play as a film. I explained that I was too involved with *Tender*

*Mercies* to think about another film. They asked to read it, and liked it, but when they tried to initiate its production, they had as much difficulty getting the film financed as Duvall and I had. The four of us—Duvall, the Hobels, and myself—were very particular about the director we wanted to work with. It was not easy to find someone we all wanted. A few directors we all agreed on turned it down either because they didn't like the material or because I didn't agree to the changes they asked for. The response from the studio was not overwhelmingly enthusiastic either, but nothing seemed to discourage the Hobels or destroy their belief in the project.

After many months, a friend suggested it be sent to Barry Spikings and John Cohn at EMI. Cohn immediately read the screenplay and sent word that he and Spikings were interested. They suggested Bruce Beresford as a director. Beresford called from Australia to say that he liked the screenplay and that if he could get along with the writer, he would be happy to direct. He flew to New York to meet me and we liked each other at once. Why did it take all this time to find a director and a studio willing to finance and release our production? Why did they like it without any of the reservations others seem to have had? I've learned not to question things like that, only to be grateful that they did like it.

The version of *Tender Mercies* Beresford read had several flashbacks. He had used these so effectively in *Breaker Morant* that I thought he would surely be pleased by my use of them. But no, the only change he asked for in the screenplay before filming was the elimination of the flashbacks. There were other changes during the filming, mostly cuts, or rearrangement of scenes. A few scenes were improvised between Duvall and Sonny. A particular favorite of mine is when Duvall shows Sonny how to play a guitar, because it shows in an unsentimental way the growing warmth between the two of them. During the editing, three scenes were cut that I regretted losing, but Bruce and Billy Anderson, the editor, felt that they kept the film from moving forward and so were taken out.

*Tender Mercies* was filmed in Texas in the Waxahachie area with mainly Texas crews. While there, my wife and I started to think about exploring the then-growing world of independent film production. I did a screenplay of my play *1918* and with the generous help of Lewis Allen, Peter Newman, and Ross Milloy, we were finally able to make the film the following year in Waxahachie.

While we were editing *1918* in Dallas, Pete Masterson called to say he would like to direct a film of *The Trip to Bountiful*. I'd had film offers for it ever since it was first produced as a play, but I could never agree with the producer or director on the casting of its protagonist, Mrs. Watts. Lillian Gish had created the television role in 1953 and the following season had played it with great success in the New York theater. I had thought of Geraldine Page for the part the year before Pete called me, but when a producer came to me about a production, he didn't agree with my choice and we parted company. When I mentioned Geraldine to Pete, he said she was his choice, too.

With *The Trip to Bountiful*, I was, of course, the original creator as well as the adaptor. I had done this before with *Baby, the Rain Must Fall*, *1918*, and *Valentine's Day*, but these adaptations had been done soon after the plays were produced in the theater. *The Trip to Bountiful* was a play that had been written and produced some thirty years before. In neither the play nor the television version could Mrs. Watts' trip be fully dramatized, and that was a task I set for myself in writing the screenplay. I hoped to do this without turning it into a travelogue and diluting the power of the scenes that had served so well dramatically in the earlier versions.

In my screenplay, Mrs. Watts takes a local bus from her apartment to the railroad station, then walks from the railroad station to the bus station, gets on a bus to Harrison, and finally is driven by car to her home in Bountiful. It wasn't much of a trip at all, really, and I hoped all this could be shown without sentimentality. Pete Masterson's direction and choice of location and Geraldine Page's performance all supported and strengthened my vision of that part of the film.

All the films except *Baby, the Rain Must Fall*, *To Kill a Mockingbird*, and *Tender Mercies* were independently produced and distributed. Only *To Kill a Mockingbird* was filmed in a Hollywood studio (Universal). *Baby, the Rain Must Fall, 1918, On Valentine's Day*, and *Tender Mercies* were filmed in Texas, *Courtship* and *Tomorrow* in Mississippi.

There was a time if you had asked me if I preferred writing for theater or films, I would have said, without hesitation, the theater. Now, I would hate to give up either. With the rise of independent film production, a screenwriter has increased opportunities to see his work reach the screen as he envisioned it. I'm no Pollyanna about such matters, however. The struggle of writers to be free of interference is constant, not only in films, but on Broadway and off. What was the cry of the Becks in the sixties? "Burn the scripts." And they were certainly no Hollywood tycoons.

—Horton Foote
November 1988

# To Kill a Mockingbird

# Cast

| | |
|---|---|
| ATTICUS FINCH | Gregory Peck |
| SCOUT FINCH | Mary Badham |
| JEM FINCH | Phillip Alford |
| DILL HARRIS | John Megna |
| SHERIFF HECK TATE | Frank Overton |
| MISS MAUDIE ATKINSON | Rosemary Murphy |
| MRS. DUBOSE | Ruth White |
| TOM ROBINSON | Brock Peters |
| CALPURNIA | Estelle Evans |
| JUDGE TAYLOR | Paul Fix |
| MAYELLA EWELL | Collin Wilcox |
| BOB EWELL | James Anderson |
| STEPHANIE CRAWFORD | Alice Ghostley |
| BOO RADLEY | Robert Duvall |
| GILMER | William Windom |
| WALTER CUNNINGHAM | Crahan Denton |
| MR. RADLEY | Richard Hale |
| WALTER CUNNINGHAM, JR. | Steve Condit |
| REVEREND SYKES | Bill Walker |
| Narration (JEAN LOUISE FINCH) | Kim Stanley |

# Credits

Produced by Alan J. Pakula
Directed by Robert Mulligan
Screenplay by Horton Foote, adapted from
Harper Lee's novel *To Kill a Mockingbird*
Director of Photography: Russell Harlan, A.S.C.
Music by Elmer Bernstein
Art Directors: Alexander Golitzen and Henry Bumstead
Film Editor: Aaron Stell, A.C.E.
Costumes by Rosemary Odell


A Universal presentation of a Pakula-Mulligan,
Brentwood Productions Picture

*FADE IN.*
*EXTERIOR: MAYCOMB, ALABAMA. DAYBREAK.*

*It is just before dawn, and in the half-light cotton farms, pinewoods,*
*the hills surrounding Maycomb, and the Courthouse Square are seen.*
*A young woman's voice is heard.*

JEAN LOUISE (*voice over*): Maycomb was a tired old town, even
in 1932 . . . when I first knew it. Somehow, it was hotter
then. Men's stiff collars wilted by nine in the morning.
Ladies bathed before noon and after their three o'clock
naps. And by nightfall they were like soft teacakes with
frosting from sweating and sweet talcum. The day was
twenty-four hours long, but it seemed longer. There's no
hurry, for there's nowhere to go and nothing to buy . . .
and no money to buy it with. Although Maycomb
County had recently been told that it had nothing to fear
but fear itself.

(*The Finch house and yard are seen. It is a small frame house, built*
*high off the ground and with a porch in the manner of Southern*
*cottages of its day. The yard is a large one, filled with oaks, and it has*
*an air of mystery about it in the early morning light.*)

That summer, I was six years old.

(WALTER CUNNINGHAM, *a thin, raw-boned farmer in his late fifties, comes into view. He is carrying a crokersack full of hickory nuts. He passes under the oak tree at the side of the house.* SCOUT, *six, dressed in blue jeans, drops from one of its branches to the ground. She brushes herself off and goes toward* MR. CUNNINGHAM.)

SCOUT: Good morning, Mr. Cunningham.

CUNNINGHAM: Mornin' Miss.

SCOUT: My daddy is getting dressed. Would you like me to call him for you?

CUNNINGHAM: No, Miss . . . I . . . don't care to bother.

SCOUT: Why, it's no bother, Mr. Cunningham. He'll be happy to see you. Atticus. (SCOUT *hurries up the steps and opens the door.*) Atticus, here's Mr. Cunningham.

(SCOUT *steps back onto the porch as* ATTICUS *enters.* WALTER CUNNINGHAM *seems ill at ease and embarrassed.*)

ATTICUS: Good morning, Walter.

CUNNINGHAM: Good morning, Mr. Finch. I . . . didn't want to bother you none. I brung you these hickory nuts as part of my entailment.

ATTICUS (*reaching for the sack of nuts*): Well, I thank you. The collards we had last week were delicious.

CUNNINGHAM (*gesturing, and then turning to leave*): Well, good morning.

ATTICUS: Good morning, Walter.

(ATTICUS *holds the sack of nuts.* SCOUT *is on the steps behind him.* SCOUT *leans on Atticus' shoulders as they watch* MR. CUNNINGHAM *leave.*)

Scout, I think maybe next time Mr. Cunningham comes, you better not call me.

SCOUT: Well, I thought you'd want to thank him.

ATTICUS: Oh, I do. I think it embarrasses him to be thanked.

(ATTICUS *turns and puts the sack on the porch and starts for the front yard to get the morning papers.* SCOUT *follows after him.*)

SCOUT: Why does he bring you all this stuff?

ATTICUS: He is paying me for some legal work I did for him.

SCOUT: Why is he paying you like this?

ATTICUS: That's the only way he can . . . he has no money.

(ATTICUS *comes back to the porch as* SCOUT *follows. He picks up the newspaper and reads.*)

SCOUT: Is he poor?

ATTICUS: Yes.

SCOUT: Are we poor?

ATTICUS: We are indeed.

SCOUT: Are we as poor as the Cunninghams?

ATTICUS: No, not exactly. The Cunninghams are country folks, farmers, and the crash hit them the hardest.

(CALPURNIA, *in her late fifties, appears at the screen door.*)

CALPURNIA: Scout, call your brother. (*She goes back inside.*)

SCOUT: Atticus, Jem is up in the tree. He says he won't come down until you agree to play football for the Methodists.

(ATTICUS *walks toward the tree. In a treehouse, high up in the tree, sits* JEM. *He is ten, with a serious, manly little face. Right now, he is scowling.*)

ATTICUS: Jem . . . Son, why don't you come on down and have your breakfast? Calpurnia has a good one . . . hot biscuits.

JEM: No Sir. Not until you agree to play football for the Methodists.

(ATTICUS *is looking up at* JEM. SCOUT *is swinging in the tire swing.*)

ATTICUS: Oh, no, Son. I can't do that. I explained to you I'm too old to get out there. After all, I'm the only father you have. You wouldn't want me to get out there and get my head knocked off, would you?

JEM: I ain't coming down.

ATTICUS: Suit yourself.

(ATTICUS *turns and starts for the kitchen door as he reads the newspaper.* JEM *moves out from behind the covering and watches.* SCOUT *starts to go across the street and stops by the tree.* MISS MAUDIE ATKINSON, *a strong, warm-hearted woman, keenly interested in* ATTICUS *and the children, is working on her flowers in her yard across the street.*)

MAUDIE: Good morning.

SCOUT: Good morning, Miss Maudie.

MAUDIE: What's going on over there?

SCOUT: I'm having a terrible time, Miss Maudie. Jem is staying up in that tree until Atticus agrees to play football for the Methodists, and Atticus says he's too old.

JEM: Every time I want him to do something . . . he's too old . . . He's too old for anything.

MAUDIE: He can do plenty of things.

ATTICUS (*entering the yard from the house and walking over*): You be good, children, and mind Cal. Good morning, Maudie.

MAUDIE: Good morning, Atticus.

(*Church bells ring.*)

JEM: He won't let me have a gun. He'll only play touch football with me . . . never tackle.

MAUDIE (*glancing in Atticus' direction, then looking at* JEM): He can make somebody's will so airtight you can't break it. You count your blessings and stop complaining . . . both of you.

(ATTICUS *continues on out of the yard.* MISS MAUDIE *walks away.* SCOUT *climbs up into the tree.*)

SCOUT: Jem, he is pretty old.

JEM: I can't help that.

(*He swings down to the lower limb in disgust and looks down into Miss Stephanie Crawford's collard patch next door. A boy,* DILL, *is sitting among the collards. Sitting down, he is not much higher than the collards. He has a solemn, owlish face, a knowledge and imagination too old for his years. He looks up at* JEM.)

DILL (*tentatively*): Hey . . .

JEM: Hey, yourself.

DILL (*standing up*): I'm Charles Baker Harris. I can read. You got anything needs reading, I can do it.

JEM: How old are you? Four and a half?

DILL: Going on seven.

JEM: Well, no wonder then. Scout's been reading since she was born and don't start to school till next month. You look right puny for goin' on seven.

DILL: I'm little, but I'm old. Folks call me Dill. I'm from Meridian, Mississippi, and I'm spending two weeks next door with my Aunt Stephanie. My mama works for a photographer in Meridian. She entered my picture in the "Beautiful Child Contest" and won five dollars. She gave the money to me and I went to the picture show twenty times with it.

(SCOUT *and* JEM *climb down from the treehouse.* SCOUT *climbs into the tire swing as* JEM *leans against the tree facing* DILL.)

SCOUT: Our mama's dead, but we got a daddy. Where's your daddy?

DILL: I haven't got one.

SCOUT: Is he dead?

DILL: No.

SCOUT: Well . . . if he's not dead, you've got one, haven't you?

(JEM *turns to* SCOUT.)

JEM: Hush, Scout.

(JEM *motions to her with his head as* SCOUT *whispers.*)

SCOUT: What's happened, what's up?

(CALPURNIA *enters with a shirt, and starts to dress* SCOUT.)

   Dill, this is Calpurnia.

CALPURNIA: Pleased to know you, Dill.

DILL: Pleased to know you. My daddy owns the L and N Railroad. He's going to let me run the engine all the way to New Orleans.

CALPURNIA: Is that so?

(CALPURNIA *exits.* JEM *turns away.* SCOUT *finishes putting on her shirt.*)

DILL: He says I can invite . . . anybody . . .

JEM: Shhh!

(MR. RADLEY, *in his seventies, a regal, austere man, walks by.* SCOUT *and* JEM *see him and become very subdued, as if they were afraid. Their attention leaves* DILL, *and he senses this and looks at them to see what is happening.*)

There goes the meanest man that ever took a breath of life.

DILL: Why is he the meanest man?

JEM: Well, for one thing he has a boy named Boo that he keeps chained to a bed in that house over yonder. (*Points to the house.*) See, he lives over there.

(*Moving shot: As they start to move out of the yard,* SCOUT *follows behind them. They go down the sidewalk past Miss Stephanie's house, north to the Radley house.*)

Boo only comes out at night when we are asleep and it's pitch-dark. When you wake up at night you can hear him. Once I heard him scratching on our screen door, but he was gone by the time Atticus got there.

(*They are standing by a light pole now, staring at the Radley house and yard. The house is low and was once white with a deep front porch and green shutters. But it darkened long ago to the color of the slate-gray yard around it. Rain-spotted shingles droop over the eaves of the veranda. Oak trees keep the sun away. The remains of a picket fence drunkenly guard the front yard. A "swept" yard that is never swept, where Johnson grass and rabbit tobacco grow in abundance. Dill's eyes have widened. He is becoming truly intrigued.*)

DILL: Wonder what he does in there?

SCOUT: I wonder what he looks like?

JEM: Well, judging from his tracks, he's about six and a half feet tall. He eats raw squirrels and all the cats he can catch. There's a long, jagged scar running all the way across his face. His teeth are yellow and rotten. His eyes are popped. And he drools most of the time.

DILL: Aw, I don't believe you.

(MISS STEPHANIE, *Dill's aunt, comes up behind them. She is in her late fifties—a spinster and the neighborhood gossip. She comes up without their hearing her. She has a habit of half-shouting when she talks.*)

STEPHANIE: Dill, what are you doing here?

DILL: My Lord, Aunt Stephanie, you almost gave me a heart attack.

STEPHANIE: Dill, I don't want you playing around that house over there. There's a maniac living there and he's dangerous.

JEM: See? I was just trying to warn him about Boo, and he wouldn't believe me.

STEPHANIE: Well, you'd just better believe him, Mr. Dill Harris.

JEM: Tell him about the time Boo tried to kill his papa.

STEPHANIE: Well, I was standing in my yard one day when his mama come out yelling, "He's killing us all." Turned out that Boo was sitting in the living room cutting up the paper for his scrapbook, and when his daddy come by, he reached over with his scissors, stabbed him in his leg, pulled them out, and went right on cutting the paper.

(*Dill's eyes are popping with excitement.*)

They wanted to send him to an asylum, but his daddy said no Radley was going to any asylum. So they locked him up in the basement of the courthouse till he nearly died of the damp, and his daddy brought him home. And there he is to this day, sittin' over there with his scissors . . . Lord knows what he's doin' or thinkin'.

*EXTERIOR: FINCH YARD. DAY.*

JEM *is swinging in the tire swing. In the distance the town clock is heard to strike five.*

JEM: Come on, Scout, it's five o'clock. (*Jumps from the swinging tire and starts to run out of the yard.*)

DILL: Where you going?

SCOUT: It's time to meet Atticus.

(*She runs after* JEM; DILL *follows her.*)

(*Moving shot: They run down the street.*)

DILL: Why do you call your daddy "Atticus"?

SCOUT: 'Cause Jem does.

DILL: Why does he?

SCOUT: I don't know. He just started to when he began talking.

(*They run up the street toward town.* JEM *slows down.*)

JEM: Mrs. Dubose is on her porch. (*He gestures to* DILL.) Listen, no matter what she says to you, don't answer her back. There's a Confederate pistol in her lap under her shawl and she'll kill you quick as look at you. Come on.

(*They walk cautiously on and start to pass the* DUBOSE *house. It is an old and run-down house. It has steep front steps and a dogtrot hall.* MRS. HENRY LAFAYETTE DUBOSE *sits on the front porch in her wheelchair. Beside her is a Negro girl,* JESSIE, *who takes care of her.*)

SCOUT: Hey, Mrs. Dubose.

MRS. DUBOSE (*snarling at the children*): Don't you say "hey" to me, you ugly girl. You say "good afternoon" to me. You come over here when I'm talking to you.

(SCOUT, JEM, *and* DILL *keep on going. They are made very uncomfortable by her. They see* ATTICUS *coming and run toward him.*)

JEM: Atticus, this is Dill. He's Miss Stephanie's nephew.

ATTICUS: How do you do, Dill.

MRS. DUBOSE: Listen to me when I'm talking to you. Don't your daddy teach you to respect old people? You come back here, Jean Louise Finch . . .

ATTICUS (*taking the children and walking over to her porch*): Good afternoon, Mrs. Dubose. My, you look like a picture this afternoon.

(*The children are trying to hide behind* ATTICUS. *They begin to giggle nervously at each other.*)

SCOUT (*whispering*): He don't say a picture of what.

ATTICUS (*turning to look at the yard*): My goodness gracious, look at your flowers. Did you ever see anything more beautiful? (*He gestures with hand holding hat.*) Mrs. Dubose, the gardens at Bellingrath have nothing to compare with your flowers.

MRS. DUBOSE: Oh, I don't think they're as nice as last year.

ATTICUS: Oh, I can't agree with you.

JEM (*whispering*): He gets her interested in something nice, and she forgets to be mean.

(*The three children are standing behind* ATTICUS. ATTICUS *hits* JEM *with his hat.*)

ATTICUS: I think that your yard is going to be the showplace of the town.

(*The children giggle.*)

Well, grand seeing you, Mrs. Dubose.

(*He puts on his hat. They start on.*)

*INTERIOR: SCOUT'S ROOM. NIGHT.*

*She is undressed and in bed.* ATTICUS *is seated on the bed.* SCOUT *is reading to him from* Robinson Crusoe.

SCOUT: "I had two cats which I brought ashore on my first raft, and I had a dog . . ." (*Holds the book to her face and looks at* ATTICUS.) Atticus, do you think Boo Radley ever comes and looks in my window at night? Jem says he does. This afternoon when we were over by their house . . .

ATTICUS (*interrupting*): Scout, I told you and Jem to leave those poor people alone. I want you to stay away from their house and stop tormenting them.

SCOUT: Yes Sir.

ATTICUS (*looking at his pocket watch*): Well, I think that's all the reading for tonight, honey . . . it's getting late.

(*She closes the book and he sits up and takes the book and puts it on the table.*)

SCOUT: What time is it?

ATTICUS: Eight-thirty.

SCOUT: May I see your watch?

(*He gives it to her. She opens the case and reads the inscription.*)

"To Atticus, my beloved husband." Atticus, Jem says this watch is going to belong to him some day.

ATTICUS: That's right.

SCOUT: Why?

ATTICUS: Well, it's customary for the boy to have his father's watch.

SCOUT: What are you going to give me?

ATTICUS: Well, I don't know that I have much else of value that belongs to me. But there's a pearl necklace . . . and there's a ring that belonged to your mother . . . and I've put them away . . . and they're to be yours.

(SCOUT *stretches her arms and smiles.* ATTICUS *kisses her cheek. He takes his watch and gets up. He covers her and puts out the lamp.*)

Good night, Scout.

SCOUT: Good night.

ATTICUS: Good night, Jem.

JEM (*from his room*): Good night.

(ATTICUS *goes out.*)

*INTERIOR: JEM'S ROOM. NIGHT.*

JEM *pulls the covers over himself in the darkness.*

*INTERIOR: SCOUT'S ROOM. NIGHT.*

SCOUT *lies in bed, thinking.*

SCOUT: Jem?

JEM (*off camera*): Yes?

SCOUT: How old was I when Mama died?

JEM (*off camera*): Two.

SCOUT: And how old were you?

JEM (*off camera*): Six.

SCOUT: Old as I am now?

JEM (*off camera*): Uh huh.

SCOUT: Was Mama pretty?

JEM (*off camera*): Uh huh.

*EXTERIOR: FRONT PORCH. NIGHT.*

ATTICUS *is on the front porch. He can hear the children's conversation.*

SCOUT (*off camera*): Was Mama nice?

JEM (*off camera*): Uh huh.

SCOUT (*off camera*): Did you love her?

JEM (*off camera*): Yes.

SCOUT (*off camera*): Did I love her?

JEM (*off camera*): Yes.

SCOUT (*off camera*): Do you miss her?

JEM (*off camera*): Uh huh.

(*There is silence.* ATTICUS *listens to the night sounds.* JUDGE TAYLOR, *seventy-five, comes up on the porch.*)

JUDGE: Evening, Atticus.

ATTICUS: Evening, Judge.

(*The* JUDGE *walks over to him and pulls up a chair as he starts to sit.*)

    Rather warm, isn't it?

JUDGE: Yes, indeed. (*Fans himself with his hat.*)

ATTICUS: How's Mrs. Taylor?

JUDGE: She's fine . . . fine. Thank you. (*A pause.*) Atticus, you heard about Tom Robinson?

ATTICUS: Yes Sir.

JUDGE: Grand jury will get around to chargin' him tomorrow. (*A pause.*) I was thinking about appointing you to take the case. Though I realize you're very busy these days with your practice. And your children need a great deal of your time.

ATTICUS: Yes Sir. (*Reflects thoughtfully.*) I'll take the case.

JUDGE: I'll send a boy for you tomorrow when his hearing comes up. (*The* JUDGE *rises.*) Well, I'll see you tomorrow, Atticus.

ATTICUS: Yes Sir.

JUDGE: And thank you.

ATTICUS: Yes Sir.

(JUDGE TAYLOR *leaves. Again there is silence.* ATTICUS *rocks and listens to the night sounds.*)

*EXTERIOR: FINCH PORCH. THE NEXT MORNING.*

JEM, DILL, *and* SCOUT *enter through the door.* DILL *turns to* JEM.

DILL: Hey, Jem, I bet you a "Grey Ghost" against two "Tom Swifts," you won't go any farther than Boo Radley's gate.

JEM: Aw . . .

(*They start down the steps,* JEM *in the lead.*)

DILL: You're scared to, ain't you?

JEM: I ain't scared. I go past Boo Radley's house nearly every day of my life.

SCOUT: Always running.

(JEM *and* DILL *turn to her.* JEM *shoves her.*)

JEM: You hush up, Scout. (*Starts wheeling a rubber tire.*) Come on, Dill.

SCOUT: Me first, me first . . . me first.

(JEM *stops with the tire and turns to* SCOUT.)

JEM: You've gotta let Dill go first.

SCOUT (*jumping up and down angrily*): No, no, me first.

DILL: Oh, let her go.

JEM: Scout, be still. All right, get in.

(JEM *takes hold of the tire and* SCOUT *gets inside it.*)

Hurry up.

SCOUT: All right.

JEM: You ready?

SCOUT: Uh huh. Let her go.

(*When she is inside,* JEM *suddenly pushes it with all his might.*)

(*Moving shot: It leaves the sidewalk, goes across the gravel road to the sidewalk in front of the Radley place, through the gate, up the Radley sidewalk, hits the steps of the porch, and then rolls over on its side.* DILL *and* JEM *watch this with helpless terror.* SCOUT, *dizzy and nauseated, and unaware of where she is, lies on the ground.*)

JEM (*yelling frantically*): Scout, get away from there. Scout, come on.

(SCOUT *raises her head and sees where she is. She is frozen with terror.*)

Scout, don't just lie there. Get up!

(JEM *runs to* SCOUT, *seated on the ground in front of the house.*)

Let's go.

(*He gets his sister by the hand, then looks up at the house, drops her hand, runs up the steps to the front door, touches it, comes running down, grabs the tire, takes his sister by the hand, and starts running out of the yard.*)

Run for your life, Scout. Come on, Dill!

(*Moving shot: They run out of the yard, up the sidewalk to their own yard. DILL runs fast behind them. When they get to the safety of their yard, they are all exhausted and fall on the ground. JEM is elated by his feat of touching the Radley house.*)

Now who's a coward? You tell them about this back in Meridian County, Mr. Dill Harris.

(DILL *looks at* JEM *with new respect.*)

DILL: I'll tell you what let's do. Let's go down to the courthouse and see that room they locked Boo up in. My aunt says it's bat-infested, and he almost died from the mildew. Come on. I bet they got chains and instruments of torture down there. Come on!

(DILL *runs out of the yard, as* JEM *and* SCOUT *reluctantly follow.*)

*EXTERIOR: COURTHOUSE SQUARE. DAY.*

*A group of four idlers sit lounging under some live oak trees. They watch with eagle eyes whatever happens on the square and in the courthouse.*

DILL, *followed by* SCOUT *and* JEM, *come by them.*

*One of the men,* HIRAM TOWNSEND, *recognizes* SCOUT *and* JEM. *He is in his seventies and is dressed in work clothes.*

HIRAM: Jem Finch?

JEM: Yes Sir.

HIRAM: If you're looking for your daddy, he's inside the courthouse.

SCOUT: Thank you, Sir, but we're not looking for . . .

(JEM *gives her a yank and a look and she shuts up, and they go on.*)

JEM: Thank you, Mr. Townsend, Sir.

(*They go toward the courthouse.*)

DILL: What's your daddy doin' in the courthouse?

JEM: He's a lawyer and he has a case. The grand jury is charging his client today. I heard somethin' about it when Judge Taylor came over last night.

DILL: Let's go watch.

JEM: Oh, no, Dill . . . He wouldn't like that. No, Dill . . .

(DILL *goes into the courthouse.* SCOUT *and* JEM *seem worried about following but reluctantly decide to.*)

*INTERIOR: COURTHOUSE HALL.*

*The three children enter. They look around.*

DILL: Where's your daddy?

JEM: He'll be in the courtroom. Up there.

(*Moving shot:* DILL, SCOUT, *and* JEM *solemnly climb the stairs to the second floor.*)

    Dill, wait a minute.

(*There is a small foyer here and a door leading into the courtroom. They go up to the courtroom door.*)

DILL: Is that the courtroom?

JEM: Yeah. Ssh!

DILL (*trying to look into the keyhole*): I can't see anything.

JEM: Ssh!

DILL: You lift me up so I can see what's going on.

JEM: All right. Make a saddle, Scout.

(JEM *and* SCOUT *make a packsaddle with their arms and* DILL *climbs up and peers in the glass at the top of the door.*)

DILL: Not much is happening. The judge looks like he's asleep. I see your daddy and a colored man. The colored man looks to me like he's crying. I wonder what he's done to cry about?

(DILL *gets so absorbed in watching that he stops talking.* SCOUT *and* JEM *begin to feel the strain of holding him up.*)

SCOUT: What's going on?

DILL: There are a lot of men sitting together on one side and one man is pointing at the colored man and yelling. They're taking the colored man away.

JEM: Where is Atticus?

DILL: I can't see your daddy now, either. I wonder where in the world . . .

ATTICUS (*coming out of a side door and coming toward them*): Scout. Jem. What in the world are you doing here?

(*They whirl around, dropping the startled* DILL.)

JEM: Hello, Atticus.

ATTICUS: What are you doing here?

JEM: We came down to find out where Boo Radley was locked up. We wanted to see the bats.

ATTICUS: I want you all back home right away.

JEM: Yes Sir.

ATTICUS: Run along, now. I'll see you there for dinner.

(*The three children exit down the steps.*)

(ROBERT E. LEE EWELL, *a short, bantam cock of a man, approaches* ATTICUS *and blocks his way.*)

Mr. Ewell.

EWELL: Cap'n, I . . . I'm real sorry they picked you to defend that nigger that raped my Mayella. I don't know why I didn't kill him myself instead of goin' for the sheriff. That would have saved you and the sheriff and the tax-payers a lot of trouble.

ATTICUS: Excuse me, Mr. Ewell, I'm very busy.

EWELL: Hey, Cap'n, somebody told me just now that they thought you believed Tom Robinson's story agin ours. Do you know what I said? I said you're wrong, man . . . you're clear wrong. Mr. Finch ain't takin' his story agin ours.

(ATTICUS *eyes him impassively.*)

Well, they was wrong, wasn't they?

ATTICUS: I've been appointed to defend Tom Robinson and now that he's been charged that's what I intend to do.

EWELL: You're takin' his . . .

ATTICUS: If you'll excuse me, Mr. Ewell . . .

(ATTICUS *exits as* EWELL *turns, watching him, astounded.*)

EWELL: What kind of a man are you? You got chillun of your own.

*EXTERIOR: FINCH PORCH. NIGHT.*

SCOUT *and* JEM *are sitting there.* DILL *comes running into the yard and over to them.*

DILL: Hey, Jem . . . Jem.

(JEM *goes running toward him.* SCOUT *follows. The two boys run toward Miss Stephanie's yard.* SCOUT, DILL, *and* JEM *leap over the wall separating Miss Stephanie's and Atticus' yards.*)

SCOUT (*cautiously*): I think we ought to stay right here in Miss Stephanie's yard.

JEM: You don't have to come along, Angel May.

(*The boys start to go out of Miss Stephanie's yard.* SCOUT *follows.*)

(*Moving shot: They walk down the sidewalk silently. They can hear the porch swings creaking with the weight of the neighborhood and the night murmurs of the grown people on the street. They come to the sidewalk in front of the Radley house, and* JEM *looks at the house.* DILL *and* SCOUT *stand beside him, looking too.*)

SCOUT: What are you going to do?

JEM: We're going to look in the window of the Radley house and see if we can get a look at Boo Radley. Come on, Dill.

SCOUT: Jem, please, I'm scared.

JEM (*angrily*): Then go home if you're scared. I swear, Scout, you act more like a girl all the time. Dill, come on.

(JEM *and* DILL *start on.* SCOUT *watches for a moment, then runs after them.*)

SCOUT: Wait for me. I'm coming.

JEM (*whispering*): Ssh! We'll go around the back and crawl under the high wire fence at the rear of the Radley lot. I don't believe we can be seen from there.

(*The children go on quietly to the back of the Radley property.*)

Come on!

*EXTERIOR: THE BACK OF THE RADLEY PROPERTY.*

*The fence encloses a large garden.* JEM, SCOUT, *and* DILL *come in.* JEM *holds the bottom wire up and motions* DILL *to crawl under. He does so.* SCOUT *follows. Then* SCOUT *holds up the wire for* JEM. *It is a very tight squeeze for him, but he manages to make it.*

JEM (*whispering*): Come on. Now help me. Don't make a sound.

(*The children cautiously approach the house.* SCOUT *is so intimidated by Jem's warning that she moves barely a step a minute; then, when she looks up and sees* JEM *quite a distance ahead, she begins to move faster. They reach the gate which divides the garden from the backyard.* JEM *touches it. The gate squeaks.*)

DILL (*whispering*): Spit on it!

(*The three spit on the gate hinges until they have no spit left.*)

JEM: All right.

(*The gate squeaks again.*)

SCOUT: Jem.

JEM: Ssh! Spit some more.

(*They try to muster up more spit, and then* JEM *opens the gate slowly, lifting it aside and resting it on the fence.*)

All right.

(*The backyard is even less inviting than the front. A ramshackle porch runs the width of the house. There are two doors and two dark windows between the doors. Instead of a column, a rough two-by-four supports one end of the porch. Above it a hat rack catches the moon and shines eerily.*)

Come on.

(*They cross the yard and go to the back porch.* JEM *puts his foot on the bottom step; the step squeaks. He stands still, then tries his weight by degrees. The step is silent.* JEM *skips two steps, puts his foot on the porch, heaves himself to it, and teeters a long moment. He regains his balance and drops onto his knees. He crawls to a window, raises his head, and looks in.* SCOUT *suddenly looks up and sees a shadow. It is the shadow of a man. The back porch is bathed in moonlight, and the shadow moves across the porch toward* JEM. DILL *sees it next. He puts his hands to his face. The shadow crosses* JEM. JEM *sees it. He puts his arms over his head and goes rigid. The shadow stops about a foot beyond* JEM. *Its arms come out from its sides, drop, and are still. Then it turns and moves back across* JEM, *walks along the porch and off the side of the house, returning as it had come.* JEM *leaps off the porch and gallops toward* SCOUT *and* DILL. *He pushes* DILL *and* SCOUT *through the gate and the collards.*)

> Move, move!

(JEM *holds the bottom wire of the fence, and* SCOUT *and* DILL *roll through.* JEM *starts under the fence and is caught. He struggles as the wire holds his pants.* JEM *looks up, terrified, as he tries to pull free.*)

> Scout!

(SCOUT *and* DILL *run to him.*)

> Scout!

(JEM *is on his hands and knees under the fence.* SCOUT *kneels down and tries to free Jem's pants.* SCOUT *and* DILL *remove Jem's pants as he kicks and struggles. Then he rises.*)

(*Moving shot: They run.*)

> Scout. Quick—over here.

(JEM, SCOUT, *and* DILL *continue running through the bushes behind their garage. They are frightened and breathing hard. They all fall to their knees and huddle against the garage wall. They look at one another but are unable to speak.* DILL *cannot get his breath and starts to cough.*)

Ssh! Ssh!

(DILL *buries his head in his knees.* JEM *finally gets up and peers around the corner of the garage.* SCOUT *watches him.*)

SCOUT (*whispering*): What are you going to do for pants, Jem?

JEM: I don't know.

STEPHANIE (*calling off camera*): Dill! Dill! You come on in now.

(*They all jump.* DILL *turns to the others, very frightened.*)

DILL: I'd better go.

STEPHANIE (*shouting off camera*): Dill!

DILL (*calling*): Coming, Aunt Stephanie. (*Whispering to* JEM *and* SCOUT:) So long. I'll see you next summer.

JEM: So long.

SCOUT: So long.

(DILL *runs across the driveway and climbs the fence into Miss Stephanie's yard.*)

STEPHANIE (*calling*): Dill!

DILL: I'm coming.

JEM: I'm going back after my pants.

SCOUT: Oh, please, Jem, come on in the house.

JEM: I can't go in without my pants. (*He starts to go.*)

SCOUT: Well, I'm going to call Atticus.

JEM (*grabbing her collar and wrenching it tight*): No, you're not. Now listen. Atticus ain't never whipped me since I can remember, and I plan to keep it that way.

SCOUT: Then I'm going with you.

JEM: No, you ain't. You stay right here. I'll be back before you can count to ten.

(SCOUT *watches* JEM *vault over the low fence and disappear in the high bushes. She starts counting.*)

SCOUT: One . . . two . . . three . . . four . . .

ATTICUS (*calling*): Jem. Scout. Come on in.

SCOUT (*counting*): . . . five . . . six . . . seven . . . eight . . . nine . . . ten . . . eleven . . . twelve . . . thirteen . . . fourteen . . .

(*There is a sound of a shotgun blast.* SCOUT *stands there stunned. Suddenly she shuts her eyes and presses her hands over her ears. She looks as if she's about to scream. At that moment,* JEM *bursts through the bushes and jumps the fence, crashing into* SCOUT.)

Jem!

JEM (*clapping his hand over her mouth*): Ssh! (*He begins frantically to pull on his pants.*)

(*There is the sound of dogs barking.*)

EXTERIOR: STREET IN FRONT OF THE RADLEY HOUSE.

ATTICUS *and* MISS MAUDIE *are there talking to* MR. RADLEY, *who is holding a shotgun. They both start up the street toward Miss Stephanie's house.* MISS STEPHANIE *comes running off her front porch, pulling on a robe over her nightgown.*

STEPHANIE: What's going on? What happened? What's going on? What is it? Atticus, what is it? Will somebody please tell me what's going on?

ATTICUS: Mr. Radley shot at a prowler out in his collard patch.

STEPHANIE: A prowler. Oh, Maudie . . . (*Moves to* MAUDIE, *who comforts her.*)

MAUDIE: Well, whoever it was won't be back any time soon. Mr. Radley must have scared them out of their wits.

ATTICUS: Well, good night.

STEPHANIE: Good night.

MAUDIE: Good night, Atticus.

(ATTICUS *goes toward his house, and* MAUDIE *and* STEPHANIE *go toward Stephanie's house.*)

STEPHANIE: Oh, it scared the living daylights out of me.

(ATTICUS *sees* SCOUT *and* JEM *in the yard.*)

ATTICUS: Come on in the house. The excitement is over. Time for bed. Scout. Jem.

(SCOUT *and* JEM *look at each other. Then they start for the house. As they climb the steps,* JEM *looks back over his shoulder toward the Radley house.*)

*INTERIOR: FINCH KITCHEN. THE NEXT MORNING.*

ATTICUS *and* JEM *are eating breakfast.* CALPURNIA *is serving them.* MISS MAUDIE *comes into the kitchen.*

MAUDIE: Good morning.

CALPURNIA: Good morning, Miss Maudie.

ATTICUS: Good morning, Maudie.

CALPURNIA (*going to the hall door and calling*): Scout!

MAUDIE: I came to see Jean Louise ready for her first day of school.

(CALPURNIA *gets the coffeepot from the stove.*)

Hey, Jem.

CALPURNIA (*calling*): Scout! (*Pours the coffee.*)

ATTICUS: What are you going to do with yourself all morning, Cal, with both the children in school?

CALPURNIA: I don't know, and that's the truth. I was thinking about that just now. (*Goes back to the hall door and calls.*) Scout! Scout! Did you hear me, Scout? Now hurry!

(CALPURNIA *comes back in, and* SCOUT *follows. She has on a dress and feels very awkward in it.* JEM *sees her.*)

JEM: Hey, everybody . . . look at Scout!

(*He is about to make a comment and laugh, but* MISS MAUDIE *gives him a poke.*)

MAUDIE: Ssh!

ATTICUS: Come on in, Scout.

(JEM *giggles.*)

Have your breakfast.

MAUDIE: I think your dress is mighty becoming, honey.

(SCOUT *is not reassured; she begins to tug at it.* MISS MAUDIE *nods her head to* ATTICUS *to let him know she approves of the dress.*)

CALPURNIA: Now, don't go tugging at that dress, Scout. You want to have it all wrinkled before you even get to school?

SCOUT: I still don't see why I have to wear a darn old dress.

MAUDIE: You'll get used to it.

(SCOUT *sits at the table and starts to eat.* JEM *has eaten his break-fast—all he's going to—and gets up.*)

JEM: I'm ready.

ATTICUS: Jem! It's half an hour before school starts. Sit right down and wait for your sister.

JEM (*returning to the table and sitting*): Well, hurry up, Scout.

SCOUT: I'm trying to. (*Takes a few halfhearted bites, then gets up.*)

JEM: Well, come on . . . it's your first day. Do you want to be late?

SCOUT: I'm ready.

JEM: Come on, let's go.

(JEM *exits as* SCOUT *drops her books in the doorway. She picks them up and then runs to* ATTICUS *and kisses his cheek. She runs out the door as* JEM *runs in, grabbing his books.*)

SCOUT: Bye.

JEM: Goodbye, everyone!

(MISS MAUDIE, ATTICUS, *and* CALPURNIA *go as far as the screen door with them.* SCOUT *and* JEM *go out of the screen door.*)

*EXTERIOR: SCHOOL GROUNDS.*

SCOUT *sees* WALTER CUNNINGHAM, JR., *seven, standing in the school yard. She grabs him, throws him down, and begins to rub his nose in the dirt.*

SCOUT: Darn you, Walter Cunningham.

(*The other children gather around, watching the fight.* WALTER *and* SCOUT *are on the ground. She pounds him on the back with her fists.* JEM *comes running up and pulls her off.*)

JEM: Cut that out! What do you think you're doing?

SCOUT: He made me start off on the wrong foot. I was trying to explain to that darn lady teacher why he didn't have no money for his lunch, and she got sore at me.

JEM (*continuing to hold her as they struggle*): Stop it! Stop it!

(*A group of children have gathered around* JEM *holding* SCOUT. *He releases her.* JEM *walks to* WALTER *as the others start to disperse.*

WALTER *has picked himself up and stands with his fists half-cocked.*
JEM *looks him over.*)

Your daddy Mr. Walter Cunningham from Old Sarum?

(WALTER *nods his head "yes."*)

Well, come home and have dinner with us, Walter. We'd
be glad to have you.

(*Walter's face brightens, then darkens.*)

Well, our daddy's a friend of your daddy's. Scout here is
crazy. She won't fight you no more.

(WALTER *stands biting his lip, thinking but not answering.*)

*INTERIOR: FINCH LIVING ROOM—DINING ROOM.*

*The living room is comfortable but unpretentiously furnished. There
are a sofa, two overstuffed chairs, and a rocker in the room. Through
an alcove the dining room can be seen. The table is set for dinner and*
JEM, SCOUT, *and* WALTER *are there with* ATTICUS. CALPUR-
NIA *is serving the food.*

ATTICUS: That's a dinner that you'll enjoy.

(WALTER *looks down at his plate. There are string beans, roast, corn
bread, turnips, and rice.* WALTER *looks at* ATTICUS.)

WALTER: Yes Sir. I don't know when I've had a roast. We've
been having squirrels and rabbits lately. My pa and I go
hunting in our spare time.

JEM: You got a gun of your own?

WALTER: Uh huh.

JEM: How long have you had a gun?

WALTER: Oh, a year or so.

(JEM *looks at* ATTICUS.)

Can I have the syrup, please?

ATTICUS: Certainly, Son. (*Calls to* CALPURNIA:) Cal, will you please bring in the syrup dish?

CALPURNIA (*calling back*): Yes Sir.

JEM: How old were you when you got your first gun, Atticus?

ATTICUS: Thirteen or fourteen. I remember when my daddy gave me that gun. He told me that I should never point it at anything in the house. And that he'd rather I'd just shoot tin cans in the backyard, but he said that sooner or later he supposed the temptation to go after birds would be too much, and that I could shoot all the blue jays I wanted, if I could hit them, but to remember it is a sin to kill a mockingbird.

JEM: Why?

ATTICUS: Well, I reckon because mockingbirds don't do anything but make music for us to enjoy. They don't eat people's gardens, don't nest in the corncribs, they don't do one thing but just sing their hearts out for us. (*Looks at* SCOUT.) How did you like school, Scout?

SCOUT: All right.

(CALPURNIA *enters with the syrup dish.*)

ATTICUS: Oh, thank you, Cal. That's for Walter.

(*She takes the dish to* WALTER. *He begins to pour it liberally all over his food.* SCOUT *is watching this process. She makes a face of disgust.*)

SCOUT: What in the Sam Hill are you doing, Walter?

(*Atticus' hand thumps the table beside her.*)

But, Atticus . . . he has gone and drowned his dinner in syrup.

*(The silver saucer clatters.* WALTER *places the pitcher on it and quickly puts his hands in his lap and ducks his head.* ATTICUS *shakes his head at* SCOUT *to keep quiet.)*

CALPURNIA: Scout!

SCOUT: What?

CALPURNIA: Come out here. I want to talk to you.

*(*SCOUT *eyes her suspiciously, sees she is in no mood to be trifled with, and goes out to the kitchen.* CALPURNIA *stalks after her.)*

*INTERIOR: KITCHEN.*

SCOUT *and* CALPURNIA *enter.*

CALPURNIA: That boy is your company. And if he wants to
    eat up that tablecloth, you let him, you hear? And if you
    can't act fit to eat like folks, you can just set here and eat
    in the kitchen. *(Sends her back into the dining room with a
    smack.)*

*INTERIOR: LIVING ROOM—DINING ROOM.*

ATTICUS, JEM, *and* WALTER *continue eating as* SCOUT *runs
through the dining room and living room to the front porch.*

*EXTERIOR: FRONT PORCH.*

SCOUT *sits on the swing.*

ATTICUS *(calling)*: Scout! *(Comes out on the porch.)* Scout.
    Scout, what in the world's got into you? Now, now . . .
    *(Sits on the swing next to her.)*

SCOUT: Atticus, I'm not going back to school anymore.

ATTICUS: Now, Scout, it's just the first day.

SCOUT: I don't care. Everything went wrong. My teacher got
    mad as the devil at me and said you were teaching me to

read all wrong and to stop it. And then she acted like a fool and tried to give Walter Cunningham a quarter when everybody knows Cunninghams won't take nothin' from nobody. Any fool could have told her that.

ATTICUS: Well, maybe she's just nervous. After all, it's her first day, too, teachin' school and bein' new here.

SCOUT: Oh, Atticus.

ATTICUS: Now, wait a minute. If you can learn a single trick, Scout, you'll get along a lot better with all kinds of folks. You never really understand a person until you consider things from his point of view.

SCOUT: Sir?

ATTICUS: Until you climb inside of his skin and walk around in it.

SCOUT: But if I keep goin' to school, we can't ever read anymore.

ATTICUS: Scout, do you know what a compromise is?

SCOUT: Bending the law?

ATTICUS: No. It's an agreement reached by mutual consent. Now, here's the way it works. You concede the necessity of goin' to school, we'll keep right on readin' every night, the same as we always have. Is that a bargain?

(SCOUT *and* ATTICUS *continue talking as Jean Louise's voice is heard.*)

JEAN LOUISE (*voice over*): There just didn't seem to be anyone or thing Atticus couldn't explain. Though it wasn't a talent that would arouse the admiration of any of our friends. Jem and I had to admit he was very good at that, but that was all he was good at, we thought.

*EXTERIOR: FINCH HOUSE. DAY.*

SCOUT *and* JEM *are playing, using sticks as guns.* SCOUT *stops and watches* JEM *for a beat.*

SCOUT: What are you looking at?

JEM: That old dog down yonder.

SCOUT: That's old Tim Johnson, ain't it? What's he doing?

JEM: I don't know, Scout. We better get inside.

(*They run into the house.*)

*EXTERIOR: FRONT PORCH OF FINCH HOUSE. DAY.*

SCOUT, JEM, *and* CALPURNIA *come out of the house onto the front porch and look down the road.*

JEM: See, there he is.

(*They see the dog, not much more than a speck in the distance, walking erratically as if his right legs were shorter than his left legs. He snarls and jumps.* CALPURNIA *turns to* JEM *and* SCOUT *and makes them go inside.*)

CALPURNIA: Scout, Jem, come on inside. Come on, come on, get in!

*INTERIOR: KITCHEN. DAY.*

CALPURNIA *and the children run into the kitchen. She goes to the telephone, shouting in her excitement.*

CALPURNIA: Mr. Finch? This is Cal. I swear to God there's a mad dog comin' down the street a piece. He's comin' this way.

*EXTERIOR: FINCH HOUSE. DAY.*

*It is quiet and deserted. A black Ford swings into the driveway.* ATTICUS *and the sheriff,* HECK TATE, *get out.* TATE *carries a heavy rifle.* CALPURNIA *comes out on the porch. She points down the street. The children stare out of the screen door. There is a total stillness.* HECK TATE *sniffs and then blows his nose. He shifts the gun to the crook of his arm.*

ATTICUS (*softly*): There he is.

(*The dog comes into sight, walking dazedly in the inner rim of a curve parallel to the Radley place.*)

TATE: He's got it all right, Mr. Finch.

(*The dog is still advancing at a snail's pace. He seems dedicated to one course and motivated by an invisible force that inches him toward the Finches'. He reaches the street which runs in front of the Radley place. He pauses as if with what is left of his poor mind he is trying to consider what road to take. He makes a few hesitant steps, reaches the Radley gate, tries to turn around, but is having difficulty.*)

ATTICUS: He's within range, Heck.

TATE: Take him, Mr. Finch.

(*He hands the rifle to* ATTICUS.)

SCOUT (*calling out*): Oh, no, Mr. Tate. He don't shoot.

ATTICUS: Don't waste time, Heck.

TATE: For God's sake, Mr. Finch, he's got to be killed right away before he starts runnin'. Look where he is. I can't shoot that well. You know it.

ATTICUS: I haven't shot a gun in twenty years.

TATE (*almost throwing the gun at* ATTICUS): I'd feel mighty comfortable if you did now.

(ATTICUS *accepts the gun. He walks out of the yard and to the middle of the street. He raises his glasses, pushes them to his forehead. They slip down, and he drops them in the street. In the silence, we can hear them crack.* ATTICUS, *blinking hard, rubs his eyes and his chin. The dog has made up his mind. He takes two steps forward, stops, raises his head. The dog's body goes rigid.* ATTICUS *brings the gun to his shoulder. The rifle cracks. The dog leaps, flops over, and crumples on the sidewalk.* HECK TATE *runs toward the Radleys'.* ATTICUS *stoops, picks up his glasses and grinds the broken lens to powder, and walks toward the dog.*)

(JEM *and* SCOUT *are dumbfounded.* SCOUT *regains her senses first and pinches* JEM *to get him moving. They run out of the door.* HECK TATE *and* ATTICUS *are walking toward the house. They meet the still awestruck* SCOUT *and* JEM. *The children approach* ATTICUS *reverently.*)

ATTICUS: Don't go near that dog, you understand? He's just as dangerous dead as alive.

JEM: Yes Sir, Atticus. Atticus?

ATTICUS: Yes, Son.

JEM: Nothin'.

TATE: What's the matter, boy? Can't you talk? Didn't you know your daddy's the best shot in this county?

ATTICUS: Oh, hush, Heck. Let's get back to town. Remember now, don't go near that dog.

JEM: Yes Sir.

TATE: I'll send Zeebo out right away to pick him up.

(*He and* ATTICUS *get into the car and drive off.* JEM *and* SCOUT, *still stunned, watch them go.*)

*EXTERIOR: FINCH GARAGE. NIGHT.*

ATTICUS *backs the car out. It is an old car, not very well kept.* SCOUT *and* JEM *come running toward him.*

JEM: Atticus, can we go with you, please?

SCOUT: Can we?

(ATTICUS *keeps the motor running and calls out of the window.*)

ATTICUS: No, I have to go to the country on business, and you'll just get tired.

SCOUT: No. Not me, I won't get tired.

ATTICUS: Well, will you promise to stay in the car while I go in and talk to Helen Robinson?

SCOUT: Uh huh.

ATTICUS: And not nag about leavin' if you do get tired?

JEM: No.

ATTICUS: All right. Climb in.

(SCOUT *and* JEM *run for the car.* JEM *gets in the backseat,* SCOUT *gets in beside her father.*)

SCOUT: Who's Helen Robinson?

ATTICUS: The wife of the man I'm defending.

(*The car moves on.* SCOUT *is asleep in the front seat in a few minutes.* ATTICUS *looks down and sees she is and pulls her closer to him.*)

*EXTERIOR: TOM ROBINSON'S HOUSE AND YARD. NIGHT.*

*It is a small, neat house and yard. Tom's son, Jem's age, is playing in the yard. Atticus' car drives up. The boy stops playing and watches the car.* HELEN ROBINSON, *twenty-nine, comes to the door of the house. She has a baby in her arms, and three small children hang on her dress.* ATTICUS *gets out of the car and goes to the porch. He calls to the boy.*

ATTICUS: Evening, David.

DAVID: Evening.

ATTICUS: Evening, Helen.

HELEN: Evening, Mr. Finch.

ATTICUS: I came over to tell you about my visit with Tom.

HELEN: Yes.

ATTICUS: And to let you know that I got a postponement.

(HELEN *holds the door open for* ATTICUS, *and they go in. The boy,* DAVID, *stares at* JEM *for a beat. They wave at each other. He then looks off toward the dirt road.* JEM *turns and looks in the same direction. Down the dirt road, drunk, toward the car, comes* BOB EWELL. JEM *is frightened and starts to leave the car, and then remembers the sleeping* SCOUT. *He climbs into the front seat beside his sister, all the while watching the approach of* EWELL.)

JEM (*calling to* DAVID): Tell my daddy to come out here, please.

(DAVID *runs into the house.*)

(JEM *gets close to* SCOUT *and watches* EWELL *get closer and closer.* EWELL *comes right up to the car and stares in the window at* SCOUT *and* JEM. *He is unshaven and looks as if he'd been on a long drunk. He is unsteady and holds on to the side of the car, staring at the two children.* ATTICUS *comes to the car.* EWELL *stares drunkenly at him.* ATTICUS *gets in the car beside* SCOUT.)

ATTICUS: No need to be afraid of him, Son. He's all bluff.

(EWELL *takes a swig of whiskey from a bottle he has taken from his back pocket and goes reeling off down the road.* JEM *climbs in the back seat.* ATTICUS *starts the car.* ATTICUS *turns the car around and goes slowly back down the dirt road. The lights of the car pick up* EWELL *standing drunkenly in the middle of the road looking like some terrible figure of wrath.* ATTICUS *has to slow the car down to almost a crawl in order to pass* EWELL *without hitting him. As he passes,* EWELL *yells.*)

EWELL: Nigger lover!

(JEM *leans across the front seat and puts his hand on his father's shoulder.* ATTICUS *senses the boy's fright and pats his hand.* SCOUT *sleeps through it all. They drive on, leaving the drunken fury of a man shouting in the darkness.*)

*EXTERIOR: FINCH HOUSE. NIGHT.*

ATTICUS *drives the car up. He glances back at* JEM.

ATTICUS: There's a lot of ugly things in this world, Son. I wish I could keep 'em all away from you. That's never possible.

(ATTICUS *leans down and lifts the sleeping* SCOUT *off the seat. He carries* SCOUT *toward the house as* CALPURNIA *comes out from the kitchen.*)

If you wait until I get Scout in bed, I'll drive you home.

CALPURNIA: Yes Sir.

(ATTICUS *starts for the house.* JEM *sits on the porch in the rocking chair.*)

ATTICUS (*coming out*): Jem, would you mind staying here with Scout until I get Cal home?

JEM: No Sir.

CALPURNIA: Night, Jem.

JEM: Night, Cal.

(JEM *sees his father and* CALPURNIA *get into the car and start off. A tree rustles, a shadow passes over the porch where* JEM *sits, a night bird calls. He is struck with sudden terror.*)

(*Moving shot: He starts to run toward the Radley place in the direction of his father's car.* JEM *runs awhile longer, past the Radley oak, calling "Atticus, Atticus." He realizes it is futile and stops. He*

*freezes. He sees something gleaming and reflecting the moonlight in
the knothole of the oak tree, where it is hollow. He stops, looks around,
sticks his hand in the knothole, and takes out a shiny medal. He
quickly puts it in his pocket. He runs past the Radley house, into his
yard, and into the house.)*

*EXTERIOR: SCHOOL GROUNDS. DAY.*

SCOUT *and two other girls are jumping rope. A boy,* CECIL
JACOBS, *who is Scout's age, pulls the rope away, ending the jumping.
He and* SCOUT *face each other in anger. Other kids group around as
they argue.* SCOUT *jumps on* CECIL *and throws him to the ground as
they fight. The other children gather around and begin yelling, egging
them on.* JEM *rushes in and pulls* SCOUT *off* CECIL, *as she struggles.*
CECIL *runs off. The other children move away.*

JEAN LOUISE (*voice over*): Atticus had promised me he would
    wear me out if he ever heard of me fightin' any more. I
    was far too old and too big for such childish things, and
    the sooner I learned to hold in, the better off everybody
    would be. I soon forgot . . . Cecil Jacobs made me forget.

*EXTERIOR: FINCH FRONT PORCH. AFTERNOON.*

SCOUT *sits on the front steps, her head buried in her arms.* ATTICUS
*comes into the yard.* SCOUT *looks up.*

ATTICUS: Well, what is it, Scout?

SCOUT: Atticus, do you defend niggers?

ATTICUS: Don't say "nigger," Scout.

SCOUT: I didn't say it . . . Cecil Jacobs did. That's why I had
    to fight him.

ATTICUS (*sternly*): Scout, I don't want you fightin'!

SCOUT: I had to, Atticus . . . He . . .

ATTICUS (*interrupting*): I don't care what the reasons are. I
    forbid you to fight.

SCOUT: Yes Sir.

(ATTICUS *sits down beside* SCOUT, *putting his hat and briefcase down on the porch.*)

ATTICUS: Anyway, I'm simply defending a Negro, Tom Robinson. Scout . . . there are some things you're not old enough to understand just yet. There's been some high talk around town to the effect that I shouldn't do much about defending this man.

SCOUT (*looking up*): If you shouldn't be defending him, then why are you doing it?

ATTICUS (*putting his arm around* SCOUT, *hugging her close to him*): For a number of reasons. The main one is if I didn't, I couldn't hold my head up in this town. I couldn't even tell you and Jem not to do somethin' again. Scout, you're gonna hear some ugly talk about this in school. But I want you to promise me one thing . . . that you won't get into fights over it, no matter what they say to you.

SCOUT (*breaking loose*): Yes Sir.

(ATTICUS *gets up and goes inside the house.* SCOUT *sees* JEM *on the sidewalk and goes toward him. He is walking most peculiarly, with his feet out and his arms held to his sides. He is doing an imitation of ancient Egyptians.* SCOUT *runs to meet him. When she gets five feet from him, she becomes aware of his peculiar walk and stops and looks more closely.*)

What are you doing?

JEM: Walking like an Egyptian. We were studyin' about them in school. Teacher says we wouldn't be no place without them.

SCOUT: Is that so?

(*She begins to try to imitate his walk. They go toward the Radleys'.*)

JEM: Cradle of civilization. They invented embalming and toilet paper . . . (*He sees her imitation. He stops and goes to her, kneels and takes her feet.*) That's wrong, Scout. You do your feet this way. (*He takes her feet and tries to fix them. He is kneeling in front of the Radley oak tree with the knothole. While he is kneeling,* SCOUT *glances around at the oak and sees two figures carved out of soap in the knothole.*)

SCOUT: Look, Jem.

(*She points to the figures and gets close beside him and peers at them. He tenderly takes the two soap figures out of the knothole. One is the figure of a boy. The other wears a crude dress.*)

Look . . . the boy has hair in front of his eyebrows like you do.

JEM: And the girl wears bangs like you . . . these are us!

(MR. RADLEY *enters from behind the tree and looks at* JEM. JEM *jumps back, frightened.* MR. RADLEY *starts filling the knothole with cement from a trowel.* JEM *and* SCOUT *stand watching him. They start to back away, and then go running down the street, as* MR. RADLEY *continues filling the hole with cement.*)

*INTERIOR: JEM'S ROOM. NIGHT.*

JEM *is seated on the bed with an open cigar box in front of him. He picks up both dolls and puts them inside the box and closes it quickly as* SCOUT *enters the room.*

SCOUT: Jem . . . are you awake?

JEM: Go back to bed!

(*She moves to the bed and sits down at the foot of it.*)

SCOUT: I can't go to sleep.

JEM: Go back to bed!

(*She notices the cigar box.*)

SCOUT: What you got in the box?

JEM: Nothin'. Go back to bed!

SCOUT: Come on.

JEM: If I show you, will you swear never to tell anybody?

SCOUT: I swear . . .

JEM: Cross your heart . . .

(*She crosses her heart with her left hand and raises it in a swearing gesture, then lowers it and waits as* JEM *takes the box and opens the top. They look in the box. There is a spelling medal, a pocket watch, some pennies, a broken pocketknife. He takes the medal out and holds it up for* SCOUT *to see. She is wide-eyed.*)

I found all these in the knothole of that ole tree . . . at different times. This is a spelling medal. You know, they used to award these in school to spelling winners before we were born. And another time I found this . . . (*He picks up the pocket watch.*) And this . . . (*He holds up the pocketknife.*) And Scout, you know something else I never told you about that night I went back to the Radleys'?

SCOUT: Something else? You never told me anything about that night.

JEM: Well . . . you know the first time when I was gittin' outta my britches?

SCOUT: Uh huh.

JEM: Well, they was all in a tangle, and I couldn't get 'em loose. Well, when I went back, though, they were folded across the fence . . . sorta like they was expectin' me.

(SCOUT *is looking at the watch. She is goggle-eyed.* JEM *holds the soap figures of the boy and the girl he found in the knothole.*)

JEAN LOUISE (*voice over*): It was to be a long time before Jem and I talked about Boo again.

*INTERIOR: FINCH KITCHEN. DAY.*

CALPURNIA *is at the sink.* SCOUT *and* JEM *are eating.* DILL *comes in.*

JEAN LOUISE (*voice over*): School finally ended and summer came . . . and so did Dill.

DILL: Good mornin'.

CALPURNIA: Good mornin'. My, you're up mighty bright and early.

DILL: Oh, I've been up since four.

CALPURNIA: Four?

DILL: Oh, yes, I always get up at four. It's in my blood. You see, my daddy was a railroad man till he got rich. Now he flies airplanes. One of these days, he's just goin' to swoop down here to Maycomb, pick me up, and take me for a ride.

*EXTERIOR: FINCH HOUSE. LATE AFTERNOON.*

ATTICUS *sits on the porch reading as* JEM *comes out with a pitcher of juice. He moves back to* ATTICUS *and puts the pitcher on the chair beside him, then he takes a cookie from a plate on the chair.* ATTICUS *lifts his briefcase and starts putting his papers inside. The Sheriff's car comes by.*

JEM: Who's that in the car with Sheriff Tate?

ATTICUS (*looking up*): Tom Robinson, Son.

JEM: Where's he been?

ATTICUS: In the Abbottsville jail.

JEM: Why?

ATTICUS: The sheriff thought he'd be safer there. They're bringin' him back here tonight because his trial is tomorrow. (*He gets up and goes into the house.*)

*INTERIOR: JEM'S ROOM. NIGHT.*

*In his room,* JEM *is lying in bed beside the sleeping* DILL. *He hears a knock at the screen door.*

*INTERIOR: LIVING ROOM. NIGHT.*

ATTICUS *goes to the door and opens it.* HECK TATE *is standing there.*

ATTICUS: Well, good evenin', Heck.

TATE: Evenin', Mr. Finch.

ATTICUS: Come in.

TATE (*coming in*): The news has gotten 'round the county about my bringin' Tom Robinson back to the jail. I heard there might be trouble from that bunch out at Old Sarum.

*INTERIOR: KITCHEN. NIGHT.*

ATTICUS *goes into the kitchen to* CALPURNIA.

ATTICUS: Cal, if I need you to stay here tonight, can you do it?

CALPURNIA: Yes Sir . . . I can.

ATTICUS: Thank you. I think you better count on stayin'.

CALPURNIA: Yes Sir.

(ATTICUS *goes out.* CALPURNIA *goes back to work.*)

*INTERIOR: JEM'S ROOM. NIGHT.*

JEM *is lying in bed, still awake.* DILL *is asleep.* ATTICUS *comes in and gets something from the shelf and goes out again.* JEM *gets out of*

*bed and listens by the door. He gets his clothes from the closet and starts
to get dressed.* DILL *awakens and sits up in bed.* SCOUT *comes into
the room.*

DILL: What's going on?

JEM: Sssh. Go back to sleep!

SCOUT: What's going on?

JEM: Sssshhh!

*(The three of them go out of the room.)*

*EXTERIOR: FINCH HOUSE. NIGHT.*

*They come outside and walk down the sidewalk toward town.*

*EXTERIOR: TOWN SQUARE. NIGHT.*

*It is deserted and dark. The stores around the square are dark except
for night lights burning back by the safes and cash registers.*

*Moving shot: The three children walk down the street by Atticus'
office. They see his car parked in front of the building. They look in the
doorway of the building. It is dark.* JEM *tries the knob of the door. It is
locked.*

JEM: Hey, there's his car.

*(They walk up the sidewalk. They see a solitary light burning in the
distance. It is from the jail. As they approach the jail, they can see the
long extension cord* ATTICUS *brought from the house running between
the bars of the second-floor window and down the side of the building.
In the light from its bare bulb they see* ATTICUS *propped against the
front door. He is sitting on one of the office chairs, and he is reading a
newspaper, oblivious of the night bugs hovering above his head.)*

See, there he is . . . over there!

*(*SCOUT *starts to run toward him.)*

No, Scout . . . don't go to him. He might not like it. I

just wanted to see where he was and what he was up to.
He's all right. Let's go back home. Come on.

*(The children start back across the square, taking a shortcut, when
they hear a noise and pause. They see four dusty cars come in from the
Meridian Highway, moving slowly, in a line. They go around the
square, pass the bank building, and stop in front of the jail. Nobody
gets out.* ATTICUS *looks up from his newspaper, closes it, deliberately
folds it, drops it in his lap, and pushes his hat to the back of his head. He
seems to be expecting the men.* SCOUT, JEM, *and* DILL *run to the
cover of some bushes and hide behind them, watching.)*

*(In ones and twos, the men get out of the cars. They are country men.*
WALTER CUNNINGHAM, SR., *is among them. They surround*
ATTICUS.)*

MAN: He in there, Mr. Finch?

ATTICUS: He is. He's asleep. Don't wake him.

CUNNINGHAM: You know what we want. Get aside from that
door, Mr. Finch.

ATTICUS: Walter, I think you ought to turn right around and
go back home. Heck Tate's around here somewhere.

KELLEY: No, he ain't. Heck's bunch is out chasin' around Ole
Sarum lookin' for us.

TEX: We knowed he was, so we came around the other way.

KELLEY: And you hadn't never thought about that, had you,
Mr. Finch?

ATTICUS: I thought about it.

*(The children run over to the car.)*

SCOUT: I can't see Atticus.

*(*SCOUT *darts out toward the men,* DILL *behind her, before* JEM *can
reach out and grab them.)*

ATTICUS: Well, that changes things, doesn't it?

(SCOUT *and* DILL *run,* JEM *behind them. They run to the men and push themselves through until they reach* ATTICUS.)

SCOUT: Atticus!

(*She smiles up at him, but when she catches the look of fear on his face, she becomes insecure.* SCOUT *looks around at the men surrounding her. Most are strangers to her.*)

Hey, Atticus . . .

(ATTICUS *gets up from his chair and begins to move slowly, like an old man, toward them.*)

ATTICUS: Jem, go home. And take Scout and Dill home with you.

(SCOUT *looks up at* JEM. *She sees he is not thinking of leaving.* JEM *shakes his head "no." Atticus' fists go to his hips and so do Jem's, and they face each other in defiance.*)

Son, I said, "Go home!"

JEM: No Sir!

(JEM *shakes his head. A burly man grabs* JEM *roughly by the collar.*)

MAN: I'll send him home!

(*The man almost yanks* JEM *off his feet.* ATTICUS *flushes. His fists clench; he reaches for* JEM. *But before he gets to him,* SCOUT *kicks the man swiftly.*)

SCOUT: Don't you touch him! Let 'im go! Let 'im go!

(*The man falls back in pain.* ATTICUS *puts his hand on her shoulder.*)

ATTICUS: That'll do, Scout.

SCOUT: Ain't nobody gonna do Jem that-a-way.

MAN (*growling in the back*): Now, you get 'em outta here, Mr. Finch.

ATTICUS: Jem, I want you to please leave.

JEM: No Sir.

ATTICUS: Jem!

JEM: I tell ya, I ain't goin'!

(SCOUT *becomes bored by this exchange; she looks back at the men. She sees a man she recognizes. She moves toward him.*)

SCOUT: Hey, Mr. Cunningham . . .

(WALTER CUNNINGHAM, SR., *does not seem to hear her.*)

> I said, "Hey," Mr. Cunningham. How's your entailment getting along?

(*The man blinks and hooks his thumbs into his overall straps. He seems uncomfortable. He clears his throat and looks away.* SCOUT *walks a little closer to him.*)

> Don't you remember me, Mr. Cunningham? I'm Jean Louise Finch. You brought us some hickory nuts early one morning, remember? We had a talk. I went and got my daddy to come out and thank you. I go to school with your boy. I go to school with Walter. He's a nice boy. Tell him "hey" for me, won't you? You know something, Mr. Cunningham, entailments are bad. Entailments . . .

(*Suddenly,* SCOUT *realizes she is the center of everyone's attention: the men, her brother,* DILL, ATTICUS. *She becomes self-conscious. She turns to* ATTICUS.)

> Atticus, I was just sayin' to Mr. Cunningham that entailments were bad but not to worry. Takes a long time sometimes . . .

(*She begins to dry up. She looks up at the country men staring at her. They are quite still.*)

What's the matter?

(*She looks at* ATTICUS. *He says nothing. She looks back at* MR. CUNNINGHAM.)

I sure meant no harm, Mr. Cunningham.

CUNNINGHAM: No harm taken, young lady. (*He moves forward and takes* SCOUT *by the shoulders.*) I'll tell Walter you said "hey," little lady. (*He straightens up and waves a big hand.*) Let's clear outta here. Let's go, boys.

(*As they had come, in ones and twos, the men straggle back into their cars. We hear doors slam, engines cough, and the cars drive off.* SCOUT, JEM, *and* DILL *watch them leave.*)

ATTICUS: Now you go home, all of you. I'll be there later.

JEM: Come on . . . come on.

(*The three children go on down the street.* ATTICUS *sits again in the chair, waiting.* TOM ROBINSON *calls out from the darkness of the jail.*)

TOM (*off camera*): Mr. Finch . . . they gone?

ATTICUS: They've gone. They won't bother you any more.

(*He sits back in his chair and continues watching.*)

*EXTERIOR: STREET IN FRONT OF FINCH HOUSE. EARLY MORNING. DAY.*

*People are coming from all parts of the county for the trial. It is like Saturday. Wagons carrying country people on the way to the trial stream past the house. Some men ride horseback.* SCOUT, JEM, *and* DILL *sit on the curb of the sidewalk watching the wagons and the horses go by.*

JEM: Morning, Mr. Stevens. How do you do?

(*A man rides by on a mule and waves to the children, and they wave back. A wagonload of ladies rides past. They wear cotton sunbonnets and dresses with long sleeves. A bearded man in a wool hat drives them. A wagonload of stern-faced citizens comes by next.*)

SCOUT: Did you ever see so many people? Just like on Saturday . . .

(JEM *suddenly gets up.*)

Where you goin'?

JEM: I can't stand it any longer. I'm goin' downtown to the courthouse to watch.

SCOUT: You better not! You know what Atticus said.

JEM: I don't care if he did. I'm not gonna miss the most excitin' thing that ever happened in this town!

(*They all look at each other and start toward town.*)

*EXTERIOR: COURTHOUSE SQUARE. DAY.*

*It is deserted, as everyone is inside watching the trial.* SCOUT, JEM, *and* DILL *come into the square. They stand looking up at the courthouse. They all start toward the entrance.* SCOUT, JEM, *and* DILL *go up the stairs toward the entrance.*

*INTERIOR: ENTRANCE HALL OF COURTHOUSE. DAY.*

*When they get to the entrance,* JEM *peeks through the hole of the door. He looks back at the other two.* REVEREND SYKES, *the black Baptist preacher, comes up the stairs. The children go over to him.*

JEM: It's packed solid. They're standin' all along the back. . . . Reverend!

SYKES: Yes?

JEM: Reverend Sykes, are you goin' upstairs?

SYKES: Yes, I am.

(*He starts up the stairs and they follow him.*)

*INTERIOR: COLORED BALCONY OF COURTHOUSE.*

REVEREND SYKES *enters the colored balcony with* JEM, DILL, *and* SCOUT. *He leads them among the black people in the gallery. Four blacks in the front row get up and give them their seats when they see them come in.*

SYKES: Brother John, thanks for holding my seat.

(*They sit down and peer over the balcony. The colored balcony runs along three walls of the courtroom like a second-story veranda, and from it the children see everything.*)

(*The jury sits to the left under long windows. Sunburned, lanky, they are nearly all farmers, but this is only natural. Townfolk rarely sit on juries. They are either struck or excused. The circuit solicitor and another man,* ATTICUS, *and* TOM ROBINSON *sit at tables with their backs to the children. Just inside the railing, which divides the spectators from the court, the witnesses sit in cowhide-bottomed chairs.* JUDGE TAYLOR *is on the bench, looking like a sleepy old shark.*)

(JEM, SCOUT, DILL, *and* REVEREND SYKES *are listening intently.*)

BAILIFF: This court is now in session. Everybody rise.

(*The* JUDGE *bangs his gavel.*)

*INTERIOR: COURTROOM. LATER.*

*The solicitor* MR. GILMER *is questioning the sheriff* HECK TATE.

TATE: On the night of August twenty-first I was just leavin' my office to go home when Bob . . . Mr. Ewell . . . come in, very excited, he was. And he said, get to his house quick as I could . . . that his girl had been raped. I got in my car and went out there as fast as I could. She was pretty well beat up. I asked her if Tom Robinson beat her like that. She said, "Yes, he did." I asked if he'd taken advantage of her and she said, "Yes, he did." That's all there was to it.

GILMER: Thank you.

(ATTICUS *is sitting behind his table, his chair skewed to one side, his legs crossed, and one arm is resting on the back of the chair.*)

JUDGE: Any questions, Atticus?

ATTICUS: Yes Sir. Did anybody call a doctor, Sheriff?

TATE: No Sir.

ATTICUS: Why not?

TATE: Well, I didn't think it was necessary. She was pretty well beat up. Something sho' happened. It was obvious.

ATTICUS: Now, Sheriff, you say that she was mighty beat up. In what way?

TATE: Well, she was beaten around the head. There were bruises already comin' on her arms. She had a black eye startin' an' . . .

ATTICUS: Which eye?

TATE: Let's see . . . (*Blinks and runs his hand through his hair. He points to an invisible person five inches in front of him.*) It was her left.

ATTICUS: Well, now, was that, was her left facing you . . . or lookin' the way that you were?

TATE: Oh, yes . . . that . . . would make it her right eye. It was her right eye, Mr. Finch. Now I remember. She was beaten up on that side of her face.

(HECK TATE *blinks again and then turns and looks at* TOM ROB- INSON *as if something had been made clear to him at the same time.* TOM ROBINSON *raises his head. Something has been made clear to* ATTICUS, *too, and he gets to his feet. He walks toward* HECK TATE.)

ATTICUS: Which side, again, Heck?

TATE: The right side. She had bruises on her arms and she showed me her neck. There were definite finger marks on her gullet.

ATTICUS: All around her neck? At the back of her throat?

TATE: I'd say they were all around.

(ATTICUS *nods to* MR. GILMER *as he sits down.* MR. GILMER *shakes his head at the* JUDGE. *The* JUDGE *nods to* TATE, *who rises stiffly and steps down from the witness stand.*)

JUDGE: Witness may be excused.

BAILIFF (*booming out*): Robert E. Lee Ewell . . .

(BOB EWELL *rises and struts to the stand. He raises his right hand, puts his left on the Bible, and is sworn in as a witness.*)

Place your hand on the Bible, please. Do you promise to tell the truth, the whole truth, and nothin' but the truth, so help you God?

EWELL: I do.

BAILIFF: Sit down.

(MR. GILMER *addresses* EWELL.)

GILMER: Now, Mr. Ewell . . . will you tell us, just in your own words, what happened on August twenty-first.

EWELL: Well, that night I was comin' in from the woods with a load of kindlin', and I heard Mayella screamin' as I got to the fence. So I dropped my kindlin', and I run into the fence. But when I got loose, I run up to the window and I seen him with my Mayella!

*(The rest of the testimony is drowned out by the people in the courtroom, who begin to murmur with excitement.* JUDGE TAYLOR *begins to bang his desk with his gavel.* HECK TATE *goes to the aisle, trying to quiet the crowd.* ATTICUS *is on his feet, whispering to the* JUDGE. *The spectators finally quiet down, and* MR. GILMER *continues.)*

GILMER: What did you do after you saw the defendant?

EWELL: I ran around the house tryin' to get in, but he done run through the front door just ahead o' me. But I seen who it was, all right. I seen him. And I run in the house and po' Mayella was layin' on the floor squallin'. Then I run for Mr. Tate just as quick as I could.

GILMER: Uh huh. Thank you, Mr. Ewell.

*(MR. GILMER sits down.* ATTICUS *rises and goes to the stand and faces* EWELL.)

ATTICUS: Would you mind if I just ask you a few questions, Mr. Ewell?

EWELL: No Sir, Mr. Finch, I sho' wouldn't.

ATTICUS: Folks were doin' a lot of runnin' that night. Let's see, now, you say that you ran to the window, you ran inside, you ran to Mayella, and you ran to the sheriff. Now, did you, during all the runnin', run for a doctor?

EWELL: There weren't no need to. I seen who done it.

ATTICUS: Now, Mr. Ewell . . . you've heard the sheriff's testimony. Do you agree with his description of Mayella's injuries?

EWELL: I agree with everything Mr. Tate said. Her eye was blacked. She was mighty beat up . . . mighty.

ATTICUS: Now, Mr. Ewell, can you . . . er . . . can you read and write?

EWELL: Yes Mr. Finch. I can read and I can write.

ATTICUS: Good . . . then will you write your name, please. Write there, and show us?

(ATTICUS *takes paper and pen out of his coat. He hands them to* EWELL. EWELL *looks up and sees* ATTICUS *and* JUDGE TAYLOR *looking at him intently.*)

EWELL: Well, what's so interestin'?

JUDGE: You're left-handed, Mr. Ewell.

(EWELL *turns angrily to the* JUDGE.)

EWELL: Well, what's that got to do with it, Judge? I'm a God-fearin' man. That Atticus Finch is tryin' to take advantage of me. You got to watch lawyers like Atticus Finch.

JUDGE (*banging his gavel*): Quiet! Quiet, Sir! Now the witness may take his seat.

(EWELL *sullenly leaves the witness stand.*)

BAILIFF: Mayella Violet Ewell . . .

(*A silence comes over the court as* MAYELLA EWELL *walks to the witness stand. She is a thick-bodied girl, accustomed to strenuous labor.*)

Put your hand on the Bible, please. Do you swear to tell the truth, the whole truth, and nothing but the truth, so help you God?

·(MAYELLA *nods.* MR. GILMER *rises and begins to question her.*)

GILMER: Now, Mayella, suppose you tell us just what happened, huh?

MAYELLA (*clearing her throat*): Well, Sir . . . I was sittin' on the porch, and . . . and he comes along. Uh, there's this old chifforobe in the yard . . . and I . . . I said, "You come up here, boy, and bust up this chifforobe, and I'll give you a nickel." So he . . . he come on in the yard and I go into the house to get him the nickel and I turn around, and 'fore I know it, he's on me . . . and I fought and hollered . . . but he had me around the neck, and he hit me again and again, and the next thing I knew, Papa was in the room, a-standin' over me, hollerin', "Who done it, who done it?"

GILMER: Thank you, Mayella. Your witness, Atticus.

(GILMER *walks away.* ATTICUS *gets up smiling. He opens his coat, hooks his thumbs in his vest, walks slowly across the room to the windows.*)

ATTICUS: Miss Mayella, is your father good to you? I mean, is he easy to get along with?

MAYELLA: He does tol'able . . .

ATTICUS: Except when he's drinking?

(*A pause. She glares at* ATTICUS.)

When he's riled, has he ever beaten you?

(MAYELLA *looks in Ewell's direction.*)

MAYELLA: My pa's never touched a hair o' my head in my life.

(*Atticus' glasses slip a little and he pushes them back on his head.*)

ATTICUS: Now, you say that you asked Tom to come in and chop up a . . . what was it?

MAYELLA: A chifforobe.

ATTICUS: Was this the first time that you ever asked him to come inside the fence?

MAYELLA (*acting confused and shrugging*): Yes.

ATTICUS: Didn't you ever ask him to come inside the fence before?

MAYELLA (*evasively*): I mighta.

ATTICUS: But can you remember any other occasion?

MAYELLA (*shaking her head*): No!

ATTICUS: You say, "He caught me and he choked me and he took advantage of me," is that right?

(MAYELLA *nods her head.*)

Do you remember his beating you about the face?

MAYELLA (*hesitating*): No, I don't recollect if he hit me. I . . . mean . . . yes! He hit me . . . he hit me!

ATTICUS (*turning*): Thank you! Now, will you identify the man who beat you?

MAYELLA (*pointing to* TOM): I most certainly will . . . sittin' right yonder.

ATTICUS: Tom, will you stand up, please? Let's let Mayella have a good look at you.

(TOM ROBINSON *rises to his feet. It is our first good look at him. He is thirty.* ATTICUS *goes to the table and picks up a water glass.*)

Tom, will you please catch this?

(ATTICUS *throws the glass.* TOM *is standing at the defense table. He catches the glass with his right hand.*)

Thank you.

(ATTICUS *walks to* TOM *and takes the glass.*)

Now then, this time will you please catch it with your left hand?

TOM: I can't, Sir.

ATTICUS: Why can't you?

TOM: I can't use my left hand at all. I got it caught in a cotton gin when I was twelve years old. All my muscles were torn loose.

(*There are murmurs from the crowd in the courtroom. The* JUDGE *pounds his gavel.*)

ATTICUS: Is this the man who raped you?

MAYELLA: He most certainly is.

ATTICUS: How?

MAYELLA: I don't know how. He done . . . it . . . (*She starts to sob.*) He just done it.

ATTICUS: You have testified that he choked you and he beat you. You didn't say that he sneaked up behind you and knocked you out cold, but that you turned and there he was. Do you want to tell us what really happened?

MAYELLA: I got somethin' to say. And then I ain't gonna say no more. (*She looks in Tom's direction.*) He took advantage of me.

(ATTICUS *glances in Mayella's direction with a grim expression. She shouts and gestures with her hands as she speaks.*)

An' if you fine, fancy gentlemen ain't gonna do nothin' about it, then you're just a bunch of lousy, yellow, stinkin' cowards, the . . . the whole bunch of you, and your fancy airs don't come to nothin'. Your Ma'am'in' and your Miss Mayellarin'—it don't come to nothin', Mr. Finch. Not . . . no . . .

(*She bursts into real tears. Her shoulders shake with angry heaving sobs.* ATTICUS *has hit her in a way that is not clear to him, but he has*

*had no pleasure in doing it. He sits with his head down.* MAYELLA
*runs as* EWELL *and a man grab her.*)

EWELL: You sit down there!

MAN: Come on, girl.

(EWELL *holds Mayella's arms and starts for his seat.* EWELL *helps*
MAYELLA *to her seat. She hides her head as* EWELL *sits down.*)

(*The* JUDGE *looks in Atticus' direction.*)

JUDGE: Atticus? Mr. Gilmer?

GILMER (*rising*): The State rests, Judge.

BAILIFF: Tom Robinson, take the stand.

(TOM *stands up and goes to the witness chair.*)

Put your hand on the Bible.

(TOM *puts his hand on the Bible.*)

Do you solemnly swear to tell the truth, the whole truth,
and nothing but the truth, so help you God?

TOM: I do.

BAILIFF: Sit down!

(*The* BAILIFF *turns away as* TOM *starts to sit.* ATTICUS *starts*
*toward the* JUDGE *and* TOM.)

ATTICUS: Tom, were you acquainted with Mayella Violet
Ewell?

TOM: Yes Sir. I had to pass her place goin' to and from the field
every day.

ATTICUS: Is there any other way to go?

TOM (*shaking his head*): No Sir. None's I know of.

ATTICUS: Did she ever speak to you?

Tom: Why, yes Sir. I'd tip m' hat when I'd go by, and one day she ask me to come inside the fence and bust up a chifforobe for her. She give me the hatchet and I broke it up and then she said, "I reckon I'll hafta give you a nickel, won't I?" And I said, "No Ma'am, there ain't no charge." Then I went home. Mr. Finch, that was way last spring, way over a year ago.

Atticus: And did you ever go on the place again?

Tom: Yes Sir.

Atticus: When?

Tom: Well, I went lots of times. Seemed like every time I passed by yonder, she'd have some little somethin' for me to do . . . choppin' kindlin', totin' water for her.

Atticus: What happened to you on the evening of August twenty-first of last year?

Tom: Mr. Finch, I was goin' home as usual that evenin' and I passed the Ewell place. Miss Mayella were on the porch like she said she were.

(*The spectators, white and colored, all lean forward. It is very quiet in the room.*)

An' she said for me to come there and help her a minute. Well, I went inside the fence and I looked aroun' for some kindlin' to work on, but I didn't see none. An' then she said to come in the house, she . . . she has a door needs fixin' . . . so I follow her inside an' looked at the door an' it looked all right, an' she shut the door. All the time I was wonderin' why it was so quiet like . . . an' it come to me, there was not a child on the place, an' I said to Miss Mayella, where are the chil'ren? An' she said, they all gone to get ice cream. She said it took her a slap year to save seb'm nickels, but she done it, an' they all gone to town.

(Tom *runs his hands over his face. He is obviously very uncomfortable.*)

ATTICUS: What did you say then?

TOM: Oh, I . . . I said somethin' like, "Why Miss Mayella, that's right nice o' you to treat 'em." An' she said, "You think so?" Well, I said I best be goin', I couldn't do nothin' for her, an' she said, oh, yes I could. An' I ask her what, and she said to jus' step on the chair yonder an' git that box down from on top of the chifforobe. So I done what she told me, and I was reachin' when the next thing I knew she . . . grabbed me aroun' the legs. She scared me so bad I hopped down an' turned the chair over. That was the only thing, only furniture 'sturbed in that room, Mr. Finch, I swear, when I left it.

ATTICUS: And what happened after you turned the chair over?

(Tom *comes to a dead stop. He glances at* ATTICUS, *then at the jury.*)

Tom? You've sworn to tell the whole truth. Will you do it? What happened after that?

TOM (*running his hand nervously over his mouth*): Mr. Finch, I got down off the chair, and I turned around an' she sorta jumped on me. She hugged me aroun' the waist. She reached up an' kissed me on the face. She said she never kissed a grown man before an' she might as well kiss me. She says for me to kiss her back.

(Tom *shakes his head with his eyes closed, as he reacts to this ordeal.*)

And I said, Miss Mayella, let me outta here, an' I tried to run, when Mr. Ewell cussed at me from the window an' says he's gonna kill her.

ATTICUS: And what happened after that?

TOM: I was runnin' so fast, I don't know what happened.

ATTICUS: Tom, did you rape Mayella Ewell?

TOM: I did not, Sir.

ATTICUS: Did you harm her in any way?

TOM: I . . . I did not, Sir.

(ATTICUS *turns and walks to his desk.* GILMER *rises and goes to the witness chair.*)

GILMER: Robinson, you're pretty good at bustin' up chif-forobes and kindlin' with one hand, aren't you? Strong enough to choke the breath out of a woman and sling her to the floor?

TOM (*meekly*): I never done that, Sir.

GILMER: But you're strong enough to.

TOM: I reckon so, Sir.

GILMER: Uh huh. How come you're so all-fired anxious to do that woman's chores?

(TOM *hesitates. He searches for an answer.*)

TOM: Looks like she didn't have nobody to help her. Like I said . . .

GILMER: With Mr. Ewell and seven children on the place? You did all this choppin' and work out of sheer goodness, boy? You're a mighty good fella, it seems. Did all that for not one penny.

TOM: Yes, Sir. I felt right sorry for her. She seemed . . .

GILMER: You felt sorry for her? A white woman? You felt sorry for her?

(TOM *realizes his mistake. He shifts uncomfortably in his chair.*)

*INTERIOR: COURTROOM. LATER—SAME DAY.*

ATTICUS *rises and walks toward the jury. They watch with no show
of emotion. As* ATTICUS *talks, he looks into the eyes of the men of the
jury as if to find one to encourage him.*

ATTICUS: To begin with, this case should never have come to
trial. The State has not produced one iota of medical
evidence that the crime Tom Robinson is charged with
ever took place. It has relied instead on the testimony of
two witnesses . . . whose evidence has not only been
called into serious question on cross-examination, but
has been flatly contradicted by the defendant. There is
circumstantial evidence to indicate that Mayella Ewell
was beaten savagely by someone who led almost exclu-
sively with his left. And Tom Robinson now sits before
you having taken the oath with his right hand, the only
good hand he possesses. I have nothing but pity in my
heart for the chief witness for the State. She is a victim of
cruel poverty and ignorance. But my pity does not
extend so far as to her putting a man's life at stake, which
she has done in an effort to get rid of her own guilt. Now,
I say guilt, gentlemen, because it was guilt that motivated
her. She has committed no crime, she has merely broken
a rigid and time-honored code of our society. A code so
severe that whoever breaks it is hounded from our midst
as unfit to live with. She must destroy the evidence of her
offense. But what was the evidence of her offense? Tom
Robinson, a human being. She must put Tom Robinson
away from her. Tom Robinson was for her a daily
reminder of what she did. And what did she do? She
tempted a Negro. She was white, and she tempted a
Negro. She did something that in our society is unspeak-
able. She kissed a black man. Not an old uncle, but a
strong, young Negro man. No code mattered to her
before she broke it, but it came crashing down on her

afterwards. The witnesses for the State, with the exception of the Sheriff of Maycomb County, have presented themselves to you gentlemen, to this court, in the cynical confidence that their testimony would not be doubted. Confident that you gentlemen would go along with them on the assumption, the evil assumption, that all Negroes lie, that all Negroes are basically immoral beings, all Negro men are not to be trusted around our women. An assumption one associates with minds of their caliber, and which is in itself, gentlemen, a lie, which I do not need to point out to you. And so, a quiet, humble, respectable Negro, who has had the unmitigated temerity to feel sorry for a white woman, has had to put his word against two white people. The defendant is not guilty, but somebody in this courtroom is. Now, gentlemen, in this country our courts are the great levelers, and in our courts all men are created equal.

*(The faces of the men of the jury haven't changed expression. Atticus' face begins to perspire. He wipes it with a handkerchief.)*

I'm no idealist to believe firmly in the integrity of our courts and in the jury system. That is no ideal to me. It is a living, working reality. Now I am confident that you gentlemen will review without passion the evidence that you have heard, come to a decision, and restore this man to his family. In the name of God, do your duty. In the name of God, believe Tom Robinson.

(ATTICUS *turns away from the jury. He walks and sits down next to* TOM *at the table.*)

*INTERIOR: BALCONY OF COURTROOM—SEVERAL HOURS LATER. NIGHT.*

JEM *is leaning on the rail of the balcony.* REVEREND SYKES *is behind him, with* DILL *sleeping next to him. The* REVEREND *fans himself with his hat.*

JEM: How long has the jury been out now, Reverend?

SYKES: Let's see. . . . (*He pulls out his pocket watch and looks at it.*) Almost two hours now.

JEM: I think that's an awful good sign, don't you?

(REVEREND SYKES *doesn't answer him.*)

*INTERIOR: COURTROOM. NIGHT.*

*The jury comes back into the courtroom.* TOM *is brought in and walks toward* ATTICUS. *The jailer unlocks the handcuffs from* TOM. TOM *sits next to* ATTICUS. *The* BAILIFF *enters the courtroom, followed by the* JUDGE.

BAILIFF: Court's now in session. Everybody rise.

(*The group in the courtroom rises. The* JUDGE *climbs to his chair and sits down. The spectators are then seated.*)

JUDGE: Gentlemen of the jury, have you reached a verdict?

FOREMAN: We have, your honor.

JUDGE: Will the defendant please rise and face the jury.

(TOM ROBINSON *rises and faces the jury.*)

What is your verdict?

FOREMAN: We find the defendant guilty as charged.

(TOM *sits down beside* ATTICUS.)

JUDGE: Gentlemen, this jury is dismissed.

BAILIFF: Court's adjourned.

(*The* JUDGE *rises and exits through the door. The crowd murmurs and begins to disperse. The jailer moves to* TOM *and puts handcuffs on him.* ATTICUS *walks with* TOM.)

ATTICUS: I'll go to see Helen first thing in the morning. I told her not to be disappointed, we'd probably lose this time.

(TOM *looks at him but doesn't answer.*)

Tom . . .

(ATTICUS *turns from the door and walks to his table. He starts to gather up the papers on his desk. He puts them in his briefcase. He starts to leave the courtroom. He walks down the middle aisle.* SCOUT *is leaning over the rail watching her father and the people below. As* ATTICUS *walks down the aisle, the Negroes in the balcony start to rise until all are standing.* SCOUT *is so busy watching* ATTICUS *that she isn't aware of this.* REVEREND SYKES *taps her on the shoulder.*)

SYKES: Miss Jean Louise . . . Miss Jean Louise.

(SCOUT *looks around.*)

Miss Jean Louise, stand up, your father's passin'.

(SCOUT *rises. The* REVEREND *puts his arm around her. Everyone in the colored balcony remains standing until* ATTICUS *exits out the courtroom door.*)

*EXTERIOR: MISS MAUDIE'S PORCH. NIGHT.*

MISS MAUDIE *is alone on her porch. She sees* ATTICUS *and the children coming down the sidewalk. She goes out to her yard.* ATTICUS *and the children come up to her.*

MAUDIE: Atticus . . . (*The children go to the porch and sit down.*) I . . . I'm sorry, Atticus.

ATTICUS: Well, thank you, Maudie.

(*A car comes down the road and stops in front of Miss Maudie's house.* HECK TATE *is at the wheel.*)

TATE: Atticus, can I see you for a minute?

ATTICUS: Would you excuse me?

(MAUDIE *nods, and* ATTICUS *moves to the car and talks to* TATE. MAUDIE *sits next to* JEM *on the steps.*)

MAUDIE: Jem.

JEM: Yes'm.

MAUDIE: I don't know if it'll help, but I want to say this to you. There are some men in this world who were born to do our unpleasant jobs for us. Your father's one of them.

(HECK TATE *drives off.* ATTICUS *stands quietly for a moment and then walks back to the steps.*)

What's the matter, Atticus?

ATTICUS: Tom Robinson's dead. They were taking him to Abbottsville for safekeeping. Tom broke loose and ran. The deputy called out to him to stop. Tom didn't stop. He shot at him to wound him and missed his aim. Killed him. The deputy says Tom just ran like a crazy man. The last thing I told him was not to lose heart, that we'd ask for an appeal. We had such a good chance. We had more than a good chance. I have to go out and tell his family. Would you look after the children, Maudie?

JEM (*starting after him*): Atticus, you want me to go with you?

ATTICUS: No Son, I think I'd better go out there alone.

JEM (*still going after him*): Atticus, Atticus, I'm goin' with you.

ATTICUS: All right, Son.

(*He waits for* JEM *to catch up to him.* MAUDIE, DILL, *and* SCOUT *stay huddled together on the steps watching them go.* ATTICUS *drives the car out of the garage and they go off.*)

*EXTERIOR: TOM ROBINSON'S HOUSE. NIGHT.*

*The house is dark and quiet, as are all the little houses near it.* ATTICUS *drives the car in and shines the headlights on the porch of the house where the* ROBINSON *family is seated and standing, talking.* SPENCE, *Tom's father, sits on the steps of the house.*

ATTICUS *and* JEM *drive up to the house.* ATTICUS *stops the car and gets out.* SPENCE *sees who it is and comes to him.*

SPENCE: Hello, Mr. Finch. I'm Spence, Tom's father.

(*They shake hands.*)

ATTICUS: Hello, Spence. Is Helen here?

SPENCE: Yes Sir. She's inside, lyin' down, tryin' to get a little sleep. We been talkin' about the appeal, Mr. Finch. How long do you think it'll take?

ATTICUS: Spence, there isn't going to be any appeal now. Tom is dead.

(HELEN ROBINSON *comes out of the front door. They all move toward her.* ATTICUS *takes off his hat.*)

Helen . . .

(HELEN *gives a little moan and falls over into the dirt of the yard.* SPENCE *and* ATTICUS *go to her. They lift her. She is crying. They half-carry her into the house as the others watch.*)

(BOB EWELL *comes up the road and stands near Atticus' car. He calls to one of the Negro children in the yard.* JEM *watches from inside the car.*)

EWELL: Boy, go inside and tell Atticus Finch I said to come out here. Go on, boy.

(*The boy goes inside the house.* EWELL *stands in front of the car. He turns and looks at* JEM. ATTICUS *comes out of the house and stands on the porch. He walks down the steps, past the Negroes, and goes to* EWELL *and stands in front of him.* EWELL *spits in Atticus' face.* ATTICUS *stares at him, wipes off his face, and starts to get into the car. He and* JEM *drive off as* EWELL *watches them angrily.*)

*EXTERIOR: FINCH HOUSE. NIGHT. AUTUMN.*

JEAN LOUISE (*voice over*): By October, things had settled down again. I still looked for Boo every time I went by the Radley place.

(SCOUT *is walking on the sidewalk by the picket fence. She turns and runs to the house.*)

*INTERIOR: SCOUT'S BEDROOM.*

*She comes in and takes her Halloween costume.*

JEAN LOUISE (*voice over*): This night my mind was filled with Halloween. There was to be a pageant representing our county's agricultural products.

*EXTERIOR: HOUSE. NIGHT.*

SCOUT, *in her Halloween costume, comes out followed by* JEM.

*Moving shot: They walk to the school building, past carriages and cars parked on the street. They exit into the building.*

JEAN LOUISE (*voice over*): I was to be a ham. Jem said he would escort me to the school auditorium. Thus began our longest journey together.

*EXTERIOR: SCHOOLHOUSE. NIGHT.*

*The carriages and cars are now gone.* JEM *is seated on the steps of the schoolhouse. He gets up, walks up the steps to open the door, and looks inside.*

JEM: Scout.

SCOUT (*off camera*): Yeah.

JEM: Will you come on. Everybody's gone.

SCOUT (*off camera*): I can't go home like this.

JEM: Well, I'm goin'. It's almost ten o'clock and Atticus will be waitin' for us.

(*He turns and comes down the steps.*)

SCOUT (*off camera*): All right. I'm comin'.

(*He turns and looks as* SCOUT *comes out of the door with her ham costume on.*)

But I feel like a fool walkin' home like this.

JEM: Well, it's not my fault that you lost your dress.

SCOUT: I didn't lose it. Just can't find it.

(*She comes down the steps to* JEM.)

JEM: Where are your shoes?

SCOUT: Can't find them either.

JEM: You can get 'em tomorrow.

SCOUT: But tomorrow is Sunday.

JEM: You can get the janitor to let you in. Come on.

(*They start out.*)

(*Moving shot: They walk into the wooded area.* JEM *stoops down and picks up sticks and hits trees with them as they walk along. It is black dark out there.*)

Here, Scout, let me hold onto you before you break your neck. (*Takes her hand as they walk.*)

SCOUT: Jem, you don't have to hold me.

JEM: Sshhhh.

SCOUT: What's the matter?

JEM: Hush a minute, Scout. (*Moves and looks to his right.*) Thought I heard somethin'. Ah, come on. (*They go about five paces when he makes her stop again.*) Wait.

SCOUT: Jem, are you tryin' to scare me?

JEM: Sshhh.

*(There is stillness except for the breathing of the children. Far away a dog howls.)*

SCOUT: You know I'm too old.

JEM: Be quiet.

SCOUT: I heard an old dog then.

JEM: It's not that. I hear it when we're walking along. When we stop, I don't hear it any more.

SCOUT: You hear my costume rustlin'. Halloween's got you. *(Moves and then stops.)* I hear it now.

*(The two of them stand still and listen.)*

I'll bet it's just old Cecil Jacobs tryin' to scare us. *(She yells.)* Cecil Jacobs is a big wet hen.

*(There is not a sound except the word "hen" reverberating.)*

JEM: Come on.

*(SCOUT and JEM start walking. JEM looks frightened. He holds his hand on Scout's head, covered by the ham costume. More than a rustle is heard now. Footsteps are heard, as if someone were walking behind them in heavy shoes. JEM presses Scout's head. They stop to listen. They can hear someone running toward them.)*

Run, Scout!

*(She takes a big step and she reels; she can't keep her balance in the dark. A form descends on her and grabs her, and she falls to the ground and rolls. From nearby, she can hear scuffling, kicking sounds, sounds of shoes and flesh scraping dirt and root. JEM rolls against her and is up like lightning, pulling SCOUT with him, but she is so entangled by the costume they can't get very far.)*

Run, Scout!

*(They are nearly to the road when Jem's hand leaves her. There is more scuffling and a dull crunching sound, and SCOUT screams. The*

*scuffling slowly dies away and then there is silence. She can see a man now. He groans and is pulling something heavy along the ground. The man walks away from her, heavily and unsteadily, toward the road.)*

*(She makes her way to where she thinks the road is.)*

*(Scout's point of view: She looks down the road to the street light. A man passes under it. He is carrying the limp body of* JEM. *The man continues on, crosses the Finch yard. The front door opens and* ATTICUS *runs down the steps.)*

*(Back to* SCOUT *as she runs to him, and he picks her up.)*

ATTICUS: What happened? What happened?

SCOUT: I swear, I don't know. I just don't know.

*(*CALPURNIA *comes out of the door.* ATTICUS *turns and carries* SCOUT *up the steps.)*

ATTICUS: You go and tell Dr. Reynolds to come over.

CALPURNIA: Yes Sir.

*INTERIOR: JEM'S ROOM. NIGHT.*

ATTICUS *enters with* SCOUT. *He puts* SCOUT *down in the front of Jem's room.* JEM *is lying on the bed.*

ATTICUS: You all right?

SCOUT: Yes Sir.

ATTICUS: Are you sure?

SCOUT: Yes Sir.

*(*ATTICUS *rises and leaves the room.* SCOUT *turns and looks at* JEM *lying on the bed.)*

*INTERIOR: HALL. NIGHT.*

ATTICUS *goes to the phone.* SCOUT *runs to* ATTICUS.

ATTICUS: Sheriff Tate, please.

SCOUT: Atticus, is Jem dead?

ATTICUS: No, he's unconscious. We won't know how bad he's hurt until the doctor gets here. (*Talking on the phone.*) Heck? Atticus Finch. Someone's been after my children.

*INTERIOR: JEM'S ROOM. NIGHT.*

*Jem's door is slightly open.* CALPURNIA *opens the door all the way for* DR. REYNOLDS. ATTICUS *and* SCOUT *are there.* DR. REYNOLDS *enters and examines* JEM.

DR. REYNOLDS: He's got a bad break, so far as I can tell, like somebody tried to wring his arm off. I'll be right back, Atticus.

*EXTERIOR: PORCH. NIGHT.*

DR. REYNOLDS *goes out of the front door.* TATE *comes on the porch with the ham costume.*

TATE: How's the boy, Doc?

DR. REYNOLDS: He'll be all right.

*INTERIOR: JEM'S ROOM. NIGHT.*

TATE *is at the door of Jem's room. The room is dim. Jem's reading light is shaded with a towel.* JEM *lies on his back, asleep. There is an ugly mark on the side of his face. His left arm is out from the side of his body. The man who brought* JEM *stands in a corner, leaning against the wall.* ATTICUS *is by Jem's bed.* SCOUT *and* HECK TATE *come in.*

ATTICUS: What is it, Heck?

(TATE *runs his hands down his thighs. He looks around the room.*)

TATE: Bob Ewell's lyin' on the ground under that tree down yonder with a kitchen knife stuck up under his ribs. He's dead, Mr. Finch.

(ATTICUS *gets up from the bed. He looks shocked.*)

ATTICUS: Are you sure?

TATE: Yes Sir. He ain't gonna bother these children no more. Miss Scout, you think you could tell us what happened?

(SCOUT *goes to* ATTICUS. *He puts his arms around her.*)

SCOUT: I don't know. All of a sudden somebody grabbed me. Knocked me down on the ground. Jem found me there and then Mr. Ewell, I reckon, grabbed him again, and Jem hollered. Then somebody grabbed me. Mr. Ewell, I guess. Somebody grabbed him, and then I heard someone pantin' and coughin'. Then I saw someone carrying Jem.

TATE: Well, who was it?

SCOUT: Why, there he is, Mr. Tate. He can tell you his name . . .

(*She points to the man in the corner who brought* JEM *home. He leans against the wall. He has a pale face and his hair is thin and dead white, and as she points to him, a strange spasm shakes him. At this moment, it comes to* SCOUT *who he is, and she gazes at him in wonder as a timid smile comes to his face.*)

Hey, Boo.

ATTICUS: Miss Jean Louise, Mr. Arthur Radley. I believe he already knows you.

(SCOUT *is embarrassed and tries to hide her embarrassment. She goes to cover* JEM *up.*)

Heck, let's go out on the front porch.

(ATTICUS *and* TATE *start out the door.* SCOUT *walks to* BOO, *standing in the corner behind the door.*)

SCOUT: Would you like to say good night to Jem, Mr. Arthur?

(*She holds out her hand and he takes it.* JEM *is lying in bed asleep as* BOO *and* SCOUT *walk to the bed.*)

You can pet him, Mr. Arthur. He's asleep. Couldn't if he was awake, though. He wouldn't let you.

(BOO *looks down at* JEM.)

Go ahead.

(*He bends down, and his hand reaches out and pats* JEM, *asleep in bed. Then he withdraws his hand from Jem's head. He straightens up, still looking down at* JEM. SCOUT *takes* BOO *by the hand.*)

*EXTERIOR: FINCH PORCH. NIGHT.*

SCOUT, *holding Boo's hand, opens the door and they both come out on the porch.* ATTICUS *and* TATE *are there.*

SCOUT: Let's sit in the swing, Mr. Arthur.

(SCOUT *and* BOO *walk to the swing and they sit down in it.*)

ATTICUS: Heck, I guess that the thing to do is . . . good Lord, I must be losing my memory. I can't remember whether Jem is twelve or thirteen. Anyway, it'll have to come before the County Court. Of course, it's a clear case of self-defense. I'll . . . well . . . I'll run down to the office . . .

TATE: Mr. Finch, you think Jem killed Bob Ewell? Is that what you think? Your boy never stabbed him.

(ATTICUS *looks up.* BOO *and* SCOUT *are seated in the swing.* SCOUT *looks up at* BOO.)

Bob Ewell fell on his knife. He killed himself. There's a black man dead for no reason, and now the man responsible for it is dead. Let the dead bury the dead this time, Mr. Finch. I never heard tell that it's against the law for a citizen to do his utmost to prevent a crime from being committed, which is exactly what he did. But maybe you'll tell me it's my duty to tell the town all about it, not to hush it up. Well, you know what'll happen then. All the ladies in Maycomb, includin' my wife, will be knockin' on his door bringin' angel food cakes. To my way of thinkin', takin' one man who's done you and this town a great service, and draggin' him, with his shy ways, into the limelight, to me, that's a sin. It's a sin, and I'm not about to have it on my head. I may not be much, Mr. Finch, but I'm still Sheriff of Maycomb County, and Bob Ewell fell on his knife.

(ATTICUS *looks over at* BOO. *Tate's meaning dawns on him.*)

Good night, Sir.

(TATE *goes down the steps of the porch and to his car.* SCOUT *and* BOO *are still seated in the swing.* SCOUT *gets up and walks over to* ATTICUS.)

SCOUT: Mr. Tate was right.

ATTICUS: What do you mean?

SCOUT: Well, it would be sort of like shooting a mockingbird, wouldn't it?

(ATTICUS *hugs her to him.* BOO *walks over to Jem's window, bends over, and looks inside.* ATTICUS *walks over to* BOO *at the window. They shake hands.*)

ATTICUS: Thank you, Arthur. Thank you for my children.

(ATTICUS *turns and walks into the house.* BOO *and* SCOUT *go off the porch.*)

(*Moving shot: They walk along the sidewalk. They turn in at the Radley gate and go up the front walk.*)

JEAN LOUISE (*voice over*): Neighbors bring food with death, and flowers with sickness, and little things in between.

Boo was our neighbor. He gave us two soap dolls, a broken watch and chain, a knife, and our lives.

(*They go up the steps and onto the porch to the front door.* BOO *opens the door and goes inside.*)

One time Atticus said you never really knew a man until you stood in his shoes and walked around in them. Just standin' on the Radley porch was enough.

(*Moving shot:* SCOUT *turns and walks down the steps of the porch.*)

The summer that had begun so long ago had ended, another summer had taken its place, and a fall, and Boo Radley had come out.

(SCOUT *turns at the gate and looks back at the house. She turns and goes down the walk.*)

I was to think of these days many times; of Jem, and Dill, and Boo Radley, and Tom Robinson . . .

INTERIOR: JEM'S ROOM. NIGHT.

ATTICUS *and* SCOUT *are inside Jem's room on Jem's bed.*

. . . and Atticus. He would be in Jem's room all night. And he would be there when Jem waked up in the morning.

FADE OUT.

# Tender Mercies

# $Cast$

| | |
|---:|:---|
| MAC SLEDGE | Robert Duvall |
| ROSA LEE | Tess Harper |
| DIXIE | Betty Buckley |
| HARRY | Wilford Brimley |
| SUE ANNE | Ellen Barkin |
| SONNY | Allan Hubbard |
| ROBERT | Lenny Von Dohlen |
| REPORTER | Paul Gleason |
| LEWIS MENEFEE | Michael Crabtree |
| REVEREND HOTCHKISS | Norman Bennett |
| LARUE | Andrew Scott Hollon |
| MAN IN BAR | Jerry Biggs |
| CONCESSIONAIRE | Sheila Bird |
| BOY AT DANCE | Robert E. Blackburn III |
| DOORMAN | Eli Cummins |
| MAN AT MOTEL | Tony Frank |
| MAN AT DIXIE'S HOUSE | Berkley H. Garrett |
| WOMAN WITH GROCERIES | Helena Humann |
| NURSE | Suzanne Jacobs |
| COUNTRY WOMAN | Barbara Jones |
| COUNTRY MAN | Jerry Jones |

| | | |
|---|---|---|
| WAITER | | Harlan Jordan |
| CHOIRMASTER | | Robert P. Kelley |
| MAN IN BAR/RESTAURANT | | Ray LePere |
| MAN AT DIXIE'S HOUSE | | Pat Minter |
| ADA, DIXIE'S DRESSER | | Terry Schoolcraft |
| MAN AT DIXIE'S HOUSE | | Oliver Seale |
| CONCESSIONAIRE | | Denise Simek |
| CONCESSIONAIRE | | Robert Stewart |
| WOMAN AT DANCE | | Susan Aston |
| WOMAN AT DANCE | | Vicki Neff |
| WOMAN AT DANCE | | Pamela Putnam |
| JAKE | | Rick Murray |
| BERTIE | SLATER | Stephen Funchess |
| STEVE | MILL BOYS | Glen Fleming |
| HENRY | | James Aaron |

# Credits

Produced by Philip S. Hobel
Directed by Bruce Beresford
Screenplay by Horton Foote
Director of Photography: Russell Boyd
Art Director: Jeannine Oppewall
Film Editor: William Anderson
Associate Producer: Mary-Ann Hobel
Co-Producers: Horton Foote and Robert Duvall
Costumes by Elizabeth McBride

An Antron Media production presented by E.M.I.
Distributed by Universal Pictures and
Associated Film Distribution Corp.

*FADE IN.*
*EXTERIOR: SMALL RURAL TEXAS MOTEL. NIGHT.*

*A small house of five rooms where the owner of the motel,* ROSA LEE, *and her son* SONNY *live, and three small cabins that she rents to transients. From one of these cabins the drunken brawling of two men,* MAC SLEDGE *and his roommate, is heard. Their silhouetted figures as they argue can be seen behind the curtains of their cabin.*

ROOMMATE: Yeah, give me the bottle.

MAC: Go to hell!

ROOMMATE: Goddamn you!

MAC: Get your own bottle!

ROOMMATE: Give me the bottle!

(SONNY *steps outside the house. He stands listening to the shouting.*)

Give it to me!

*EXTERIOR: CABIN.*

*The two figures cross the window again, one of the figures pausing and drinking from a bottle. Their loud bickering continues.*

MAC: I'm giving you nothing.

ROOMMATE: Give me the bottle.

MAC: I'm giving you nothing.

(ROSA LEE *comes out of her house to investigate the source of the shouting.*)

ROOMMATE: Give . . .

(ROSA LEE *places a hand on Sonny's shoulder.* SONNY *looks at her.*)

Give me the bottle.

(ROSA LEE *glances down at* SONNY.)

MAC: I'm giving you nothing.

(SONNY *and* ROSA LEE *stand listening.*)

ROOMMATE: Give me the bottle!

(MAC *and his* ROOMMATE *struggle in silhouette.*)

MAC: Come on and . . .

ROOMMATE: Give me the bottle! Give me the bottle!

*INTERIOR: CABIN. NIGHT.*

MAC *falls to the floor.*

*EXTERIOR: MOTEL. NIGHT.*

*The silhouette of the* ROOMMATE *leaves the cabin.* SONNY *and* ROSA LEE *return to their house.*

*INTERIOR: CABIN. DAY.*

MAC *slowly rises to his knees, leans on the bed, and then hauls himself onto it.*

MAC (*voice over, singing*):
    See that cloud, there in the sky
    Slowly drifting by

Well, that's the way she's
adrift from me.

(MAC *struggles over to the window. He draws back a curtain to see outside, and watches as* ROSA LEE *walks round the front of a truck to pump gas.*)

Too long I've lied . . .

WOMAN (*in truck*): Good morning.

MAC (*voice over, singing*): . . . to myself

ROSA LEE: Hi. What can I get you?

MAN (*in truck*): Think five dollars will do it.

(MAC *continues to look through the curtains at* ROSA LEE *and her customers.*)

MAC (*voice over, singing*):
    I know there's someone else

WOMAN: Gotten so high, hasn't it?

ROSA LEE: Yes, it has.

MAN: Should have been keeping it for ourselves instead of shipping up to . . .

(ROSA LEE *places hose in gas tank of truck while the* MAN *stands by and watches.*)

MAC (*voice over, singing*):
    But, oh, it hurts so much to face

MAN: . . . Yankees to squander.

(MAC *closes curtain and walks from the window.*)

MAC (*voice over, singing*):
    . . . reality.
    A little child, boy or girl

Will dream and play in their
own dream world

(MAC *goes to a mirror where he studies himself.*)

*EXTERIOR: MOTEL. DAY.*

MAC (*voice over, singing*):
And as they play
They pretend that they believe

MAN (*paying* ROSA LEE *for the gasoline*): Forty cents short of
making it. (*He turns to woman.*) You got forty cents in your
purse?

WOMAN: Let me see. (*She opens her purse.*) Here you are. (*Hands*
ROSA LEE *the difference.*)

ROSA LEE: Thank you.

*INTERIOR: CABIN. DAY.*

MAC (*voice over, singing*):
Well, I'm no child
But at times it's true

(MAC *picks his cap up from the table, puts it on, and walks to the
door.*)

*EXTERIOR: MOTEL. DAY.*

MAC (*voice over, singing*):
I pretend I'm not . . .

(ROSA LEE *is walking to the back of her truck as* MAC *steps out of his
cabin.*)

. . . losing you
Because it hurts so . . .

(ROSA LEE *walks to her house.*)

. . . much to face . . .

(MAC *walks toward* ROSA LEE *at the entrance of her house.*)

. . . reality.

ROSA LEE: Your friend said to tell you he had to move on.

MAC: How long have I been here?

ROSA LEE: Two days.

MAC: How far is it to the nearest town?

ROSA LEE: Four miles.

(*He turns and looks behind him.*)

MAC: The fellow I was with pay for the room before he left?

ROSA LEE (*standing on the porch of her house*): No.

(MAC *walks back toward his room.*)

MAC (*voice over, singing*):
. . . I'll go on . . .

(ROSA LEE *goes inside her house.*)

. . . loving you

*INTERIOR: CABIN. DAY.*

MAC *enters the room.*

Through eternity
But, oh, it hurts so much to
face reality.

(MAC *picks up his jacket from the bed and rummages through its pockets. He tosses it back down on the bed. Next he grabs a bottle lying beside it and takes hard gulps from it.* MAC *drops the bottle on bed and walks out the door.*)

*EXTERIOR: MOTEL. DAY.*

SONNY *plays on the grass with his toys as* MAC *walks behind him and approaches* ROSA LEE, *who is on the porch of her house.*

MAC: Lady, I'm broke. But I'll be glad to work out what I owe you.

ROSA LEE: All right, but there's no drinking while you're working here.

MAC: Yes Ma'am.

ROSA LEE: Are you hungry?

MAC: Well, I—I could eat something, yeah.

(ROSA LEE *goes into her house as* MAC *comes and sits down on the edge of the porch in silence.*)

*EXTERIOR: ROADSIDE. DAY.*

MAC *is collecting litter from the roadside and putting it in plastic bags.*

*INTERIOR: CABIN. DAY.*

ROSA LEE *picks up the mess left by* MAC *and his* ROOMMATE. *A radio is heard in the background.*

*EXTERIOR: MOTEL. DAY.*

MAC *repairs a door of one of the cabins as* SONNY *plays behind him.*

*EXTERIOR: MOTEL. LATER IN DAY.*

SONNY *is helping* ROSA LEE *collect the wash from the line.*

ROSA LEE: Sure is a pretty day, isn't it, Sonny?

SONNY: Yes Ma'am.

ROSA LEE: Wish I had time to stay out here in the yard and enjoy it a little bit.

(MAC *is sitting alone on the porch of Rosa Lee's house, watching them.*)

SONNY: Why don't you?

ROSA LEE: Well, I can't, honey. I've got a million things to do today.

SONNY: I'll help you.

ROSA LEE: Oh, I know you will.

*INTERIOR: ROSA LEE'S HOUSE. DAY.*

ROSA LEE *is sorting the wash.* SONNY *is doing his homework.* MAC *walks up to the door and pauses, then he knocks on the door-frame.* ROSA LEE *looks up from her work.*

ROSA LEE: Yes?

MAC: If you still need help the next couple of days, I'd like to work on.

ROSA LEE (*glancing at* SONNY): All right, I can give you your room and your meals, and two dollars an hour.

MAC: Thank you.

(MAC *nods and turns to leave.* ROSA LEE *continues to fold clothes and looks again at* SONNY, *who returns to his homework.*)

*EXTERIOR: MOTEL. DAY.*

*A car is there getting gas.* MAC *is working the pump.* MAC *replaces gas hose in the pump and walks to the driver's side to collect money. He counts the money as the car drives off. A radio is heard in the background playing country music.* ROSA LEE *steps out of the house.* MAC *stands, thoughtful for a moment, then goes to* ROSA LEE *and hands her the money.*

*INTERIOR: KITCHEN—ROSA LEE'S HOUSE. NIGHT.*

ROSA LEE, SONNY, *and* MAC *sit at the table having their meal.*

SONNY: Mister, what's your name?

MAC: Mac.

*EXTERIOR: FIELD. DAY.*

SONNY *throws stones as he walks toward* MAC, *who sits on a log.*

MAC: Don't throw stones at me, Sonny.

(SONNY *now plays with a stone rather than throwing it.*)

How was school?

SONNY: All right.

MAC: Did you learn anything?

SONNY: Not much. What are you doing down here?

MAC: Thinking.

SONNY: About what?

MAC: Things.

SONNY: Good things or bad things?

MAC: Some of both.

(SONNY *throws a stone away from them both.*)

SONNY: You never knew my daddy, did you?

MAC: I never did.

SONNY: Think you would've liked him if you'd known him?

MAC: Sure. What do you think?

SONNY: I guess.

*EXTERIOR: MOTEL. NIGHT.*

*A trailer, where* MAC *now lives, is parked outside the motel. He is inside playing a guitar and singing.*

MAC (*singing*):
    I'll learn to live alone again

*INTERIOR: TRAILER. NIGHT.*

MAC *with his guitar. He continues to play and sing.*

MAC (*singing*):
> I'll learn to love again, somehow
> I'll even learn to play the fool again.

*INTERIOR: LIVING ROOM OF ROSA LEE'S HOUSE. NIGHT.*

ROSA LEE *sits listening to Mac's song then gets up and walks to the door.*

MAC (*singing*):
> No, I never even meant to say
> goodbye to the woman that I've
> known for so long

*EXTERIOR: ROAD. DAY.*

MAC, SONNY, *and* ROSA LEE *sit in silence as the truck they are in goes down the road.*

*INTERIOR: CHURCH. DAY.*

ROSA LEE *and other choir members are singing as the* CHOIR DIRECTOR *leads them.*

CHOIR AND CONGREGATION (*singing*):
> We have heard the joyful sounds
> Jesus saves, Jesus saves
> Spread the tidings all around
> Jesus saves, Jesus saves
> Spread the news to every land
> Climb the steps and cross the waves

*EXTERIOR: CHURCH. DAY.*

CHOIR AND CONGREGATION (*off camera, singing*):
> Onward is Our Lord's command

*INTERIOR: CHURCH. DAY.*

*The* CONGREGATION *continues to sing.*

*Angle:* MAC *and* SONNY *singing along with* CHOIR *and* CON-
GREGATION.

MAC AND SONNY (*singing*):
> Jesus saves, Jesus saves
> Sing ye islands of the sea
> Echo back ye ocean caves
> Earth shall keep her jubilee
> Jesus saves, Jesus saves

(*Angle:* REVEREND HOTCHKISS, *the pastor of the church, and the*
CHOIR DIRECTOR.)

CHOIR AND CONGREGATION (*singing*):
> Shout salvation full and free
> Highest hills and deepest caves
> This our song of victory
> Jesus saves, Jesus saves.

*EXTERIOR: CHURCH STEPS. DAY.*

REVEREND HOTCHKISS *greets the congregation as they come out
of the church.*

MAN: Good to see you, Sir.

SECOND MAN: Very nice.

HOTCHKISS: See you at the midweek service.

(ROSA LEE, SONNY, *and* MAC *come up to* REVEREND
HOTCHKISS.)

> Well, hi, Sonny.

SONNY: Hi.

HOTCHKISS (*shaking hands with* ROSA LEE): How are you
doing?

ROSA LEE: Reverend, I want you to meet Mac Sledge, who
works for me down at the motel.

MAC: How do you do, Sir.

HOTCHKISS: How do you do, Mr. Sledge. (*To* ROSA LEE:) Sonny tells me he wants to be baptized. I know that makes you proud, Rosa Lee.

ROSA LEE: Yes, it does.

HOTCHKISS: You were baptized in this church, weren't you?

ROSA LEE: Yes Sir, I was.

HOTCHKISS: And where were you baptized, Mr. Sledge?

MAC: I haven't been baptized.

HOTCHKISS (*laughing*): Well, we'll have to work on you, then!

MAC: Yes Sir.

(SONNY, ROSA LEE, *and* MAC *start on.*)

HOTCHKISS: So long, Sonny, see you later.

*EXTERIOR: MOTEL. NIGHT.*

*T.V. is heard coming from Rosa Lee's house.*

*INTERIOR: LIVING ROOM—ROSA LEE'S HOUSE. NIGHT.*

MAC *and* ROSA LEE *are seated on the couch as they watch T.V.* SONNY *lies on floor watching.*

ROSA LEE: Turn off the T.V., Sonny, and get to bed. You've got school tomorrow.

SONNY: Can I talk with you all a little bit first?

ROSA LEE: No Sir.

(SONNY *reluctantly switches off the T.V. and goes to his bedroom.*)

SONNY: Good night.

ROSA LEE: Good night.

MAC: Good night. He's a good little fellow.

ROSA LEE: He's growing up so fast, he'll be gone before I know it.

MAC: Do you have any other family?

ROSA LEE: No. I was the only child my mother and daddy had. They had me kind of late in life. My daddy's been dead . . . oh, he died two years after my husband was killed and Mama died a year and a half ago last spring.

MAC: My mama and daddy are dead, too. But I have a brother out in California some place. We lost track of each other. I have a daughter.

ROSA LEE: You do?

MAC: She's seven or eight years older than your boy.

ROSA LEE: Where is she?

MAC: With her mama. Me and her mama are divorced. We didn't get along too well, and I reckon my . . .

*INTERIOR: SONNY'S BEDROOM. NIGHT.*

SONNY *lies awake in bed overhearing the talking.*

SONNY (*breaking in*): Will you all stop talking! I can't get to sleep!

*INTERIOR: LIVING ROOM—ROSA LEE'S HOUSE. NIGHT.*

ROSA LEE *and* MAC *on couch.* MAC *laughs at Sonny's request.*

*EXTERIOR: MOTEL VEGETABLE GARDEN. DAY.*

MAC *and* ROSA LEE *in the garden; he is digging with a hoe and she is weeding.*

MAC: I haven't had a drink in two months. I think my drinking is behind me.

ROSA LEE: Do you? I'm glad. I don't think it gets you anywhere.

MAC: You ever thought about marrying again?

ROSA LEE: Yes, I have. Have you?

MAC: I thought about it, lately. I guess it's no secret how I feel
about you. A blind man could see that. (*Leaning on hoe.*)
Would you think about marrying me?

ROSA LEE: Yes, I will.

(MAC *resumes his gardening, and so does* ROSA LEE.)

*EXTERIOR: SCHOOL PLAYING FIELDS. DAY.*

SONNY, *walking to recover a baseball, meets a gang of older boys.*

BOY: Hey, your dad's dead.

SONNY: I know he's dead. I know that. He got killed in
Vietnam.

BOY: What was his name?

SONNY: Carl Herbert Wadsworth. I was named after him.
I'm Carl Herbert Wadsworth, Jr.

BOY: Well, how come everybody calls you Sonny?

SONNY: I don't know. They just do.

BOY: That man your mama's married to ain't your daddy.

SONNY: I know that, dummy. I know what he is. He's my
step-daddy.

BOY: Is he still a drunk?

(SONNY *starts to fight the boy who says this.*)

*EXTERIOR: MOTEL. DAY.*

*The school bus drives up, and* SONNY *gets out, walking by* ROSA LEE *as she is pumping gas for a customer.*

ROSA LEE: Hi, how was school?

SONNY: O.K. Did my daddy go to the same school I go to?

ROSA LEE: Yes.

SONNY: Do I look like my daddy?

*EXTERIOR: CEMETERY. DAY.*

*Rosa Lee's truck is there.* MAC, SONNY, *and* ROSA LEE *are in the truck.* SONNY *and* ROSA LEE *get out.*

ROSA LEE: Coming with us, Mac?

MAC: You go on. I'll wait here.

(ROSA LEE *and* SONNY *walk to grave of his father.*)

ROSA LEE: Here it is. I couldn't put down the day he died because the army didn't know.

SONNY: Was there a big crowd at his funeral?

ROSA LEE: Yes, there was.

SONNY: Did I go?

ROSA LEE: No.

SONNY: Why not?

ROSA LEE: Because you were too little.

SONNY: Did people cry at the funeral?

ROSA LEE: Yes, they did.

SONNY: Did you?

ROSA LEE: Yes, I did.

(SONNY *looks at grave bearing the inscription:*)
          CARL HERBERT WADSWORTH
          FEBRUARY 12TH, 1951
          MAY, 1971

*EXTERIOR: MOTEL. DAY.*

*A man gets out of his car as* MAC *comes to serve him.*

MAC: Morning.

REPORTER: Fill it up.

(MAC *takes the hose and starts filling the tank with gas.*)

     Mr. Sledge?

MAC: Yes Sir.

REPORTER: Are you Mac Sledge, the singer?

MAC: Yes. I was a singer, I mean, and I am Mac Sledge.

REPORTER: You were married to Dixie Scott, weren't you?

MAC: I've got nothing to say about that.

REPORTER: She never got married again, did she? Are you
     remarried? (*He sees* SONNY *next to motel.*) Is that your
     boy? That's not your boy, is it? Mr. Sledge, it took me
     quite a while to track you down. I'd really appreciate an
     interview.

MAC: I've got nothing to say to anybody. (*Replaces the gas hose
     and starts toward the house.*)

REPORTER (*following* MAC): Well, are you doing any singing
     anymore, or writing any songs these days? Somebody
     said that your new wife is singing at the Baptist Church.
     (*A radio plays in the background.*) I guess your daughter by
     your first wife has got to be going on eighteen by now,
     huh? Hey, I'm going to do a story, Mr. Sledge. You ought

to talk to me at least to make sure I get it right. You've got two minutes. Won't you sit down and talk to me?

MAC: No Sir. (*Calling.*) Sonny!

*INTERIOR: ROSA LEE'S HOUSE. DAY.*

MAC *walks into the living room followed by the* REPORTER.

REPORTER: People around here know who you are? Your ex-wife is singing over in Austin in the next couple of nights, did you know that? You going to go over and see her? Maybe your daughter'll be along. Maybe she'll come over here and see you. Does she know where you are? Well, Dixie told me a lot about you. Don't you want to tell me a few things about her? She said alcohol is what licked you. Do you still drink?

*EXTERIOR: MOTEL. DAY.*

REPORTER *leaves the house and goes to his car.* MAC *walks into the backyard as the* REPORTER *leaves in his car.* MAC *walks further on and looks out over the newly plowed field.*

*INTERIOR: KITCHEN OF ROSA LEE'S HOUSE. NIGHT.*

MAC *and* SONNY *sit at table as* MAC *strums his guitar.* ROSA LEE *works in kitchen.*

SONNY: They say you were a rich man once.

MAC: Who says?

SONNY: Kids at school said they read it in the paper.

MAC: I don't know if I was what you call rich, but I had a few dollars.

SONNY: How did you get it?

MAC: Writing songs.

SONNY: Well, how do you get money for that?

MAC: Well, people crazy enough to pay you for it, they do it.

SONNY: What happened to your money?

MAC: I lost it.

SONNY: How?

MAC: How? Too much applejack.

SONNY: You think you'll ever be rich again?

MAC: Well, I'll tell you what, Sonny. I don't lay awake at nights worrying about it. (*He begins to play chords on the guitar.*) Now look, there's a "D," right? "D" as in "dog." Now, watch me. I'll call them out. (*Singing as he plays and showing chords to* SONNY.)
 I've decided to leave forever.

(*He looks over at* ROSA LEE *and smiles.*)

 Not really.

(*He looks back at the guitar and* SONNY *as he continues singing.*)

 Let me know if you're staying behind.

(*To* SONNY:) That's "A-7."
 Otherwise I'll be gone in the morning.

(*To* SONNY:) "D" as in "dog."
 Let me know if you're staying behind.

(*To* SONNY:) Now you can play a cover chord or a rhythm chord. (*Singing.*)
 Let me know—

(*To* SONNY:) That's a "G"—
 If you always will want me
 or if you'll wander into another's arms.

(*To* SONNY:) "A" or "A-7." "G"—
 Let me know what you decide, dear,

and let me rest my head for a while.
I've decided to leave here forever—
(*To* SONNY:) "D" as in "dog."
Let me know if you're coming along.
Otherwise, I'll be gone in the morning—
Let me know if you're staying behind.

*EXTERIOR: MOTEL. DAY.*

*Van pulls in motel parking lot and stops in front of Mac and Rosa Lee's house. A singing group called* SLATER MILL BOYS *get out. They are* JAKE, ROBERT, HENRY, STEVE, *and* BERTIE. *They wait at the van as* ROSA LEE *comes out of the house.*

ROBERT: Hi.

ROSA LEE: Hi. What can I get you?

ROBERT: Oh, about five dollars worth of gas, please.

(ROSA LEE *starts to put gas in van.* BOYS *stare at one another until* ROBERT *finally goes to rear of van as their spokesman. The others bunch up behind him.*)

　　Excuse me. Is this where Mac Sledge stays?

ROSA LEE: Yes.

ROBERT: Is he here?

ROSA LEE: Yes.

ROBERT: Well, can we talk to him?

ROSA LEE: What about?

ROBERT: We just want to meet him.

HENRY: We're admirers of his.

ROBERT: We saw the story in the newspaper this morning and
　　we've got a band.

HENRY: We'd just like to say hello and pay our respects.

JAKE: We've got all his records.

HENRY: We grew up on his music.

BERTIE: He's great.

ROSA LEE: That's five dollars.

STEVE (*to* JAKE): Come on, pay up.

BERTIE: I bought the beer.

HENRY: I paid for the gas last time. It's your turn.

ROBERT: It's his turn. Jake, give them the money.

BERTIE: Pay up.

(JAKE *pays for the gas.*)

ROBERT: Well, could we see him?

ROSA LEE: I'll ask.

SLATER MILL BOYS: All right!

(ROSA LEE *walks back to the motel office in her house. In a moment* MAC *steps outside and* ROSA LEE *follows.*)

MAC: Hello, boys.

ROBERT: Hello, Sir.

STEVE, BERTIE, AND HENRY: Howdy.

ROBERT: I was telling this lady here that . . .

MAC: Oh, this is my wife, Rosa Lee.

ROBERT: Pleased to meet you, Ma'am.

STEVE, JAKE, AND HENRY: Howdy, Ma'am.

BERTIE: Pleased to know you, Ma'am.

ROBERT: We were saying we've got a band, you know, and . . .

MAC: You five boys?

ROBERT: Yes Sir. I'm the manager. I play the guitar, and Bertie's on bass, Steve's on the fiddle, and Henry plays the steel, and Jake's drums.

MAC: Who does your vocals?

ROBERT: Well, we all take turns on that.

BERTIE: You've been a real inspiration to us all.

MAC: That's most gratifying to hear.

JAKE: When are you going to start singing again, Sir?

MAC: I'm not going to start singing again, Son. I've lost it.

JAKE: You don't miss singing?

MAC: No. Oh, I miss some things, but I don't miss a lot of it. So, maybe we'll come and listen to you some night. (*Starts walking toward motel office in the house.*)

ROBERT: We sure would like that. Hey, we wonder if you have any advice for us.

MAC: No, I don't really. Just, you know, sing it the way you feel it. Pleased to know you.

SLATER MILL BOYS (*leaving*): Nice to meet you. Nice to meet you. Goodbye. So long.

*EXTERIOR: GRAPEVINE OPERA HOUSE. NIGHT.*

*Upbeat country music is heard from inside.*

*INTERIOR: GRAPEVINE OPERA HOUSE. NIGHT.*

*All seats in the opera house are filled.* DIXIE SCOTT *and her band are on stage.*

DIXIE (*singing*):
>It's a cozy place for sleeping lazy nights
>I shut the door for a little peace and quiet
>But the best part of all
>The room at the end of the hall
>That's where you and me
>Make everything all right
>We can't afford good wine or pink champagne
>We ain't got no open fireplace flame
>But we celebrate the happiness we've found
>Every night in the best bedroom in town
>Every night in the best bedroom in town.

(*Angle: Audience in auditorium applauding.*)

(*Angle:* MAC *is in the audience; he is unenthusiastic.*)

> Thank you. Thank you very much.

(DIXIE *starts to sing another song.*)

(*Angle:* DIXIE *as she sings.*)

>Any fool can see that love is blind
>Here I am to prove it one more time
>Forget about my pride
>I didn't mean to catch you by surprise
>I hope that isn't pity in your eyes
>I've tried so hard to stay away and keep you off my
>mind
>I know I should
>But it's no good
>'Cause time goes by and I'm not over you
>I'd gladly be a fool in love again

(*Angle:* MAC *as he gets up and leaves as* DIXIE *continues singing.*)

>If there's a chance that you might see me
>Touch me, want me, ever need me,

Cause I'm still going crazy over you.
I know I'm never getting over you.

*INTERIOR: FOYER OF OPERA HOUSE. NIGHT.*

*Two* WOMEN *stand talking to a* MAN *at the box office as* MAC *walks by to the exit.*

WOMAN: It's been a long night.

MAN: Really?

WOMAN: Yeah. You better believe it.

MAN: How do you like it?

*INTERIOR: AUDITORIUM OF OPERA HOUSE. NIGHT.*

DIXIE (*singing*):
    One more cup of coffee, then I'll go
    But there's one more thing
    I think you ought to know
    The days go by and nothing's changed
    I'm still here for the taking
    And just a touch would mean so much
    To one whose heart is breaking over you.

*EXTERIOR: STREET. BACKSTAGE DOOR TO AUDITO-RIUM. NIGHT.*

MAC *is there.*

HARRY SILVER, *Dixie's manager, comes out of door backstage to meet* MAC. *Dixie's singing can still be heard in background.*

HARRY: Mac.

MAC: Hello, Harry. Good to see you.

HARRY: What are you doing around here?

MAC: Oh, I live around here.

HARRY: You do? Things going all right for you?

MAC: Pretty well.

(*A* SECURITY GUARD *steps outside and stands beside them with his arms folded.*)

HARRY: You want to see the show? It's started, but I can get you in there.

MAC: No, thanks. (*Takes an envelope out of his coat pocket.*) Harry, I have a song here. I thought you might give it to Dixie to look it over. If she likes it, maybe she'll record it.

HARRY (*taking envelope and putting it in his jacket*): All right, Mac. Kind of a surprise. I thought maybe you'd quit the business.

MAC: I have. But I just wrote this song and I thought, you know . . .

HARRY: I'll see that she gets it. You working?

MAC: At a motel.

(*Dixie's singing stops.*)

DIXIE (*off camera, very faint*): Thank you very much. Thank you . . . Thank you.

HARRY (*shaking hands with* MAC): Mac, it's good to see you. You look great and . . .

MAC: Thank you.

HARRY: . . . good luck to you. (*He returns inside.*)

DIXIE (*off camera*): Thank you, ladies and gentlemen. A big, warm, Texas welcome to Billy Bob Anderson and his Blue Jays!

(*Off camera: the song, "Overnight Sensation," starts.*)

*INTERIOR: BACKSTAGE AUDITORIUM. NIGHT.*

MAC *slowly walks down the backstage corridor. There are a number of famous country and western singers' portraits on the wall, including Mac's. He pauses to look at his photograph. Then he continues on, stopping momentarily in the doorway to Dixie's dressing room, then walks to the room across from hers as* DIXIE *enters the hallway, stopping as she sees* MAC. *She is followed by* ADA, *Dixie's dresser.*

DIXIE: What the hell are you doing here?

MAC: I was hoping to say hello to Sue Anne.

*INTERIOR: DIXIE'S DRESSING ROOM.*

DIXIE *enters, followed by* ADA *and* MAC.

DIXIE (*to* ADA): Get Harry in here right away.

(ADA *leaves.*)

> You stay away from her, do you hear me? You stay away from her or, I warn you, I'll have the law on you. All she remembers about you is a mean drunk, trying to beat up her mama. You're dead as far as she's concerned, Mac.

(ADA *returns.*)

MAC: How have you been?

DIXIE: She never thinks about you. She's happy. So leave her alone.

(HARRY *enters.*)

MAC: Lady, you're not telling me what to do. You never have and you never will.

DIXIE: Harry, get him out of here! I do not want him around!

MAC: Who the hell does she think she is? She comes out here and starts yelling at me.

DIXIE: He is jealous of me because I am successful and he's not. That's the way it's always been.

MAC: Bullshit!

DIXIE (*as* MAC *leaves*): Bullshit! (*To* HARRY:) Make sure he gets out of here and make sure that he does not see Sue Anne, O.K.?

HARRY: All right.

DIXIE: Just make sure he does not see Sue Anne, you under-stand me? O.K.?

HARRY: All right, all right, settle down.

DIXIE: "Settle down"! How? How? You know sometimes! . . . Jesus Christ!

*EXTERIOR: MOTEL. NIGHT.*

MAC *drives up in the truck, parks, and goes inside.*

*INTERIOR: LIVING ROOM OF ROSA LEE'S HOUSE. NIGHT.*

ROSA LEE *is doing the ironing.* MAC *enters.*

ROSA LEE: You're home early.

MAC (*walking into their bedroom*): Uh huh.

ROSA LEE: Concert must not have been very long.

MAC (*from bedroom*): It was the regular time. I left early.

ROSA LEE (*as* MAC *reenters*): Why?

MAC: I didn't care for it.

ROSA LEE: Why not?

MAC (*looking toward Sonny's room*): Is Sonny in bed?

ROSA LEE: Uh huh.

MAC: What have you been doing?

ROSA LEE: Not much.

MAC: You watch T.V.?

ROSA LEE: No.

MAC: Why are you so quiet? Are you mad about something? My God, woman, don't tell me you're jealous! Rosa Lee, are you jealous of Dixie Scott?

ROSA LEE: Maybe I am.

MAC: Why?

ROSA LEE: Because, you know . . .

MAC: No, I don't know.

ROSA LEE: Well, because she's rich and famous and you used to be married to her.

MAC: My God, don't be jealous of her, Rosa Lee. She's poison to me. She is absolutely poison to me.

ROSA LEE: Then why did you go and listen to her sing?

MAC: Someday I'll tell you.

ROSA LEE: Why can't you tell me now?

MAC: Because I can't.

ROSA LEE: Why not?

MAC: Because I can't.

ROSA LEE: Why?

MAC: Because I can't. Goddammit, don't you understand English?

ROSA LEE: I understand English and you don't have to yell at me. You'll wake up Sonny. Look, Mac, if you went hoping to see your daughter, I could understand that. I mean, you can come right out and tell me that.

MAC: I'd be lying to you if I told you that was the reason.

ROSA LEE: Why, didn't you want to see her?

MAC: 'Course I did. And I tried to, but Dixie saw me, and she pitched a fit.

ROSA LEE: How long has it been since you saw her?

MAC: Since before the divorce. Seven or eight years.

*EXTERIOR: MOTEL. DAY.*

MAC *and* HARRY *are talking.* ROSA LEE *stands to one side, listening.*

HARRY (*giving* MAC *envelope*): Mac, Dixie told me to bring that back to you myself and to tell you it ain't no good. She told me to tell you even if it was any good, she wouldn't sing it, and she don't want nothing more to do with you.

MAC: Now, wait. I don't want anything to do with her either. I just wrote this song. I thought it was a good song for her. I guess I was wrong. Now, did you get a look at it?

HARRY: Yeah, I looked at it.

MAC: Well, what do you think?

HARRY: Well, I don't think it's no good either. It's a different game now, Mac.

MAC: Well, that's fine.

HARRY: How are you doing?

MAC: I'm all right.

HARRY: You makin' a living here?

MAC: We get by. (*Looks over at* ROSA LEE.) Rosa Lee, this is an old friend of mine, Harry Silvers.

HARRY: Pleased to know you.

ROSA LEE: Thank you. Pleased to know you.

HARRY: I'm sorry Dixie` acted so ugly about you seeing Sue Anne. I wish you'd asked me about it first. Maybe I could have done something about it. I still think I can if you still want to see her after Dixie gets over being stubborn.

MAC: How is Sue Anne?

HARRY: She's grown up. Of course, Dixie spoils the life out of her. But you can't blame her. She's all she's got, you know. Well, nice to meet you, Mrs. Sledge.

ROSA LEE: Thank you. Nice to meet you.

HARRY: So long, Mac. Good luck.

MAC: Good luck to you.

(HARRY *goes to his car, starts it, and leaves.*)

I don't give a goddamn about any of this no more, so what in hell is wrong with me? Goddammit!

(ROSA LEE *touches his hand.*)

I guess it's hearing about Sue Anne grown up and all and being spoiled. Goddammit!

ROSA LEE: It's got to be hard on you not being able to see her. I love you, you know. And every night when I say my prayers and I thank the Lord for his blessings and his tender mercies to me, you and Sonny head the list.

MAC: Thank you.

ROSA LEE: Would you sing the song you wrote to me?

MAC: It's no good.

ROSA LEE: I sure would like to hear it.

MAC (*following her into house*): All right, but it's kind of corny.

ROSA LEE: I don't care.

MAC: Well, you asked for it.

*INTERIOR: ROSA LEE'S HOUSE. DAY.*

MAC *and* ROSA LEE *enter.*

ROSA LEE: Let me get your guitar for you.

(ROSA LEE *gets the guitar and returns.* MAC *takes the guitar.*)

MAC: Let's see. (*He starts to play a few chords on the guitar and then begins to sing.*)
> Baby, you're the only dream
> I've ever had that's come true
> There's so much more to reach
> for, thanks to you
> All I've had is me till now . . .

(*Putting down his guitar.*) I got no voice. Anyway, I don't like the song. Never have and I never will.

ROSA LEE: Mac.

MAC: Now, don't feel sorry for me, Rosa Lee, I'm not dead, you know.

ROSA LEE: I don't feel sorry for you. (*He goes out. She calls after him.*) Mac!

*EXTERIOR: MOTEL. DAY.*

MAC *comes out of motel, gets into their truck, and leaves as* ROSA LEE *follows him onto porch and watches him race off.*

*EXTERIOR: HIGHWAY. DAY.*

*Mac's truck speeds along the road.*

*EXTERIOR: CAFE. DAY.*

MAC *drives up and parks outside the cafe. He goes inside.*

*INTERIOR: CAFE. DAY.*

MAC *enters. Jukebox music can be heard in the background.* MAC *goes to the counter. The* WAITER *goes to him. There are several other men seated at the counter.*

WAITER: What do you want?

MAC: I don't know.

WAITER: You want a beer, you want food, or do you want a drink?

MAC: I don't know yet. When I do know, I'll let you know.

FIRST CUSTOMER: Pass the sugar, please.

(MAC *slides it to him angrily.*)

Thank you.

(SECOND CUSTOMER *goes to the jukebox and puts money in the slot.*)

MAC: Would you mind not playing that damn music?

SECOND CUSTOMER: Hell, yes, I mind.

(MAC *gets up and walks out of cafe.*)

What's wrong with him?

WAITER: I don't know.

*EXTERIOR: ROAD. DAY.*

MAC *is in his truck driving behind another truck. He blows his horn in anger, weaves, and finally attempts to pass the truck.*

MAC (*shouting at truck driver*): Get over, you redneck bastard. (*Races ahead, almost colliding with a car at intersection. To driver of that car:*) What are you doing, you dumb son-of-a-bitch?

DRIVER (*yelling back*): Are you crazy? What's the matter with you?

*EXTERIOR: MOTEL. DAY.*

ROSA LEE *comes out to greet* SLATER MILL BOYS, *who are there in their van.*

ROBERT (*getting out of van*): Hi. Mr. Sledge around?

ROSA LEE: No, he's not here right now. To tell you the truth, I don't know where he is and I'm not real sure when he's coming back.

ROBERT: Well, I just wanted to holler at him if he was here. We're playing at a dance round here this Saturday night, and I was wondering if we could leave one of our posters with you. (*Gets poster from* JAKE.) Give me that. (*Hands her the poster.*)

ROSA LEE: Oh, sure.

ROBERT: Thanks.

*EXTERIOR: LIQUOR STORE. NIGHT.*

MAC *parks his truck outside the store.*

MAC (*voice over, singing*):
    Sometimes, some things are hard . . .

*EXTERIOR: MOTEL. NIGHT.*

ROSA LEE *walks to roadside.*

MAC (*voice over, singing*):
    . . . to face
    With me, it's reality

Now, someone will take my place
I'll go on loving you . . .

*EXTERIOR: ROAD. NIGHT.*

MAC (*voice over, singing*):
   . . . through eternity

*EXTERIOR: LIQUOR STORE. NIGHT.*

(MAC *leaves the store with a bottle and goes to his truck.*)

MAC (*voice over, singing*):
   But, oh, it hurts so much to face reality.

*EXTERIOR: MOTEL. NIGHT.*

SONNY *pulls back curtains to look outside. He can only see the deserted road.*

*INTERIOR: ROSA LEE'S HOUSE. NIGHT.*

SONNY *looks outside again. Again, he can only see the deserted road.*

*INTERIOR: ROSA LEE'S KITCHEN. NIGHT.*

ROSA LEE *is looking at sheet music.* SONNY *comes into the kitchen.*

SONNY: I wonder where Mac is.

ROSA LEE: I don't know, Sonny.

SONNY: He's older than you are. He's fifteen years older than you.

ROSA LEE: Well, that's no secret. Everybody knows that.

SONNY: I didn't know until they told me at school.

ROSA LEE: Well, I would have told you if you'd asked me.

SONNY: Was my daddy older than you?

ROSA LEE: Yes. Two years. Let's see, I got married when I was sixteen, and I had you when I was seventeen, and I was a widow at eighteen.

SONNY: Then how come he went to Vietnam?

(*Someone drives by on road outside. They both pause to listen.*)

ROSA LEE: He got drafted. He didn't know I was going to have you till after the army got him.

SONNY: Boy at school says his daddy told him all they learned in Vietnam was to take dope. Do you think that's right?

ROSA LEE: I don't know, Sonny. I hope not.

SONNY: Do you think my daddy took drugs?

ROSA LEE: No! I don't think so.

SONNY: The kids at school take drugs.

ROSA LEE: Well, I don't want to hear of you taking them, do you hear me? If you do, I'll have your hide!

SONNY: What are you so mad about?

ROSA LEE: Never mind that. You just listen to me about them drugs.

(SONNY *gets up from table to leave.*)

Where are you going?

SONNY (*stopping at doorway*): I don't know. I sure don't want to stay around you.

ROSA LEE: All right. Look, Sonny, I'm sorry. (*Walking over to* SONNY.) Come here. Look, I didn't mean to yell at you. I'm just a little nervous tonight, O.K.?

SONNY (*pointing at sheet music*): What song is that?

ROSA LEE: That's something Mac wrote. (*Looks at the sheet music and hums part of the tune.*)

SONNY: I wish he'd come home. Where do you think he is?

Rosa Lee: I don't know, Sonny. Your guess is as good as mine.

*EXTERIOR: MOTEL. NIGHT.*

*The TV can be heard playing inside.*

*INTERIOR: ROSA LEE'S HOUSE. NIGHT.*

Rosa Lee *is watching the TV. She switches it off.*

Sonny (*off camera, calling from his bedroom*): Is he here?

Rosa Lee: No.

Sonny (*off camera*): Why did you turn off the TV?

Rosa Lee: Because I was sick of it.

Sonny (*off camera*): Going to bed?

Rosa Lee: Yes.

Sonny (*off camera*): When?

Rosa Lee: Soon. Go to sleep!

(Rosa Lee *hears another car drive past.*)

*EXTERIOR: MOTEL. NIGHT.*

Rosa Lee *opens the door and looks outside, then closes the front door.*

*INTERIOR: ROSA LEE'S HOUSE. NIGHT.*

Rosa Lee *switches off the lights in the living room and walks into Sonny's room.*

*INTERIOR: SONNY'S ROOM. NIGHT.*

*He is asleep.* Rosa Lee *enters and goes over to* Sonny *and begins stroking his hair. She starts to turn out the light, but she stops as she sees photographs of her first husband on the table. In one he is in casual clothes; in the other he is in combat fatigues. She looks at* Sonny *for a moment and then switches off the light.*

*INTERIOR: ROSA LEE AND MAC'S BEDROOM. NIGHT.*

ROSA LEE *is lying down in her bed and saying her prayers.*

ROSA LEE: Show me Thy way, O Lord, and teach me Thy path. Lead me in Thy truth and teach me. For Thou art the God of my salvation. On Thee do I wait all the day. (*Pauses as she hears a truck pull up outside. Then she hears someone enter the house through the office.*) Mac? (*Sitting up in bed.*) Is that you?

(MAC *comes to the doorway as* ROSA LEE *switches on the table lamp.*)

MAC: I'm not drunk. I bought a bottle but I poured it all out, and I'm not drunk.

ROSA LEE: Did you have anything to eat?

MAC: No.

ROSA LEE: Are you hungry?

MAC: I guess so.

ROSA LEE: Let me get you something. (*Gets out of bed and puts on a dressing gown.*) What do you want to eat? I made some soup today. You want me to heat it up?

MAC: A little soup will do me.

*INTERIOR: KITCHEN. NIGHT.*

ROSA LEE *and* MAC *are there as she prepares the soup.*

MAC: I rode by here six or seven times. I could see you all sitting here watching TV. See me ride by?

ROSA LEE: No.

MAC: I rode all over town tonight. Started twice for San Antone, turned around and came back. Started for Austin, started for Dallas, then I turned round and came back.

ROSA LEE: Do you remember that song you took over to that guy in Austin?

MAC: Yes Ma'am.

ROSA LEE: Well, remember those boys that had that band that came by here that day to see you? Well, two of them came by today, and they left off a poster. And, well, I asked them if they could read music, and one of them could, so I asked him to teach me that song you wrote, as I . . . I thought I'd try to surprise you by singing it for you when you came home.

(MAC *smiles and laughs.*)

I think it's a real pretty song, Mac. Well, and he did too. And he thought, well, he'd like his band to sing it. And I said I didn't know, I'd have to ask you. I did say I would ask, but I said you probably wouldn't care. It's an old song, it wouldn't make any difference.

MAC: Well, it's no old song, Rosa Lee. I—I only wrote it last week. That's why I got so upset when Harry said he didn't like it. (*Walks toward bedroom.*) I mean I've been writing them all along. I've even got more in here.

*INTERIOR: ROSA LEE AND MAC'S BEDROOM. NIGHT.*

MAC *enters the room and takes songs from under bed.* ROSA LEE *follows him into room.* MAC *sits on the bed.*

MAC: You say the boy liked the song?

ROSA LEE: He said he did. I sure liked it.

(MAC *gets out some song sheets.*)

What are the names of some of your other songs?

MAC: Well, one is called "The Romance Is Over" and one is called "God Can Forgive Me, Why Can't You?" (*Laughs.*) Did you learn the song?

ROSA LEE: Not well enough to sing it. I can't read music. How did you learn to read music, Mac?

MAC: I had an auntie that taught me. She had an old, half-busted piano and she sat me down at that piano all one summer when I came in from the fields and she taught me.

(MAC *starts to play guitar as* ROSA LEE *sits on bed.*)

I've been missing the music. I may not be any good anymore, but that don't keep me from missing it.

(SONNY *looks into their room. He is half-asleep.*)

SONNY: When did you get home?

ROSA LEE: He got in just a minute ago.

SONNY: You said you were going to wake me up.

MAC: Hey . . .

ROSA LEE: I forgot.

SONNY: Good night. (*Leaves.*)

ROSA LEE: Good night.

MAC: I don't care if you give that song to those boys to play.

ROSA LEE: All right.

MAC: Come on, try it with me. (*Singing.*)
　　Baby, you're the only dream I've
　　ever had that's come true.

(*Pause.*)
　　Come on.

> If you'll just hold the ladder,
> Baby, I'll climb to the top.

(*Pause.*)

> Sing it.

ROSA LEE: I can't.

MAC: Why? (*Moves the songs to one side.*) Come here. Come over here.

ROSA LEE: You just walked right out of here.

(*They embrace.*)

*INTERIOR: CLUB. NIGHT.*

The SLATER MILL BOYS *are playing.*

HENRY (*singing*):
> Drinking Canada Dry
> Since my woman said "bye."
> Yes, I'm up here in the cold
> And I want to get home,
> But I'll settle for high
> As soon as each double goes down
> I'll toast another lonely town
> This bottle's all I can see
> Till she comes back to me
> Drinking Canada Dry.

*EXTERIOR: STREET OF TOWN. DAY.*

MAC *and the* SLATER MILL BOYS *walking down the street.*

ROBERT: I call on all the radio stations. I try to get them to play our records. I've gotten to know some of those boys pretty well. I was telling them about the song, "The Ladder Song," you let us play, you know. They said we ought to try to talk you into letting us record it.

MAC (*to man seated on a bench as they pass*): Good afternoon.

ROBERT: 'Course, they thought the best idea would be to try to get you to give us another song too. And then these friends of mine said . . .

MAC: Well, I do have another song.

*INTERIOR: FEED STORE. DAY.*

MAC *and the* SLATER MILL BOYS *enter the store.*

MAC: If you come by the house, I'll let you listen to it, O.K.?

ROBERT: Thanks.

MAC (*to* SALESMAN:) How you doing?

SALESMAN: Morning.

MAC: Yes Sir, I'll have . . .

SALESMAN: What will you have?

MAC: Bag of feed.

SALESMAN: O.K.

ROBERT (*as* STEVE *is picking up bag of feed*): See, we've been at this now for four years and everybody's married but me. Jake's got a little girl too. We've still got to travel all over the state just to get engagements.

BERTIE: Yeah, we didn't clear but a hundred bucks last week.

(*They all leave the store.*)

HENRY: When we showed up down at Goliad the other night they had another band a-picking.

MAC: How many recordings did you make?

ROBERT: Three. But I haven't exactly told you the truth about that, though. They broke even on all our records.

MAC: Yeah?

ROBERT: But, even so, they're not going to record us with our own songs.

MAC: Well, it's a dirty business, but maybe it's the best thing that can happen to you for now. World isn't going to come to an end, let me tell you, if you quit playing and recording.

*EXTERIOR: STREET. DAY.*

MAC *and the* SLATER MILL BOYS *are there rounding a corner.* STEVE *carries the sack of feed.*

ROBERT: Yeah, I guess, but, like I said, we—we heard last week that they'd record us if we used two of your songs.

MAC: I gave you my permission. I told you that.

ROBERT: Yeah. But it's not just your songs. They want you to sing them.

MAC: Who does?

ROBERT: The record company.

MAC: What record company?

ROBERT: Called "The Aztec."

MAC: Never heard of it. How do you make it on a hundred a week?

ROBERT: Well, we all got other jobs. Jake's in construction, I'm a substitute teacher.

MAC (*now at his truck*): Well, I don't know.

(STEVE *throws the bag of feed into the back of the truck.*)

Thank you.

BERTIE: You bet.

MAC: Let me think about it, O.K.?

ROBERT: Sure would mean a lot to us. You understand that it'd be a real incentive for us all.

MAC: Well, I'll tell you what. I ain't promising nothing, you understand? I'll give it a try. If I don't like the way it sounds, we'll just back away from it.

ROBERT: O.K.

MAC: Give me a couple of days to think it over.

(*A* WOMAN *holding a bag of groceries comes out of the grocery store.*)

ROBERT: Thank you.

(*The* WOMAN *sees* MAC *and goes to him.*)

WOMAN: Hey, Mister! Were you really Mac Sledge?

MAC: Yes Ma'am, I guess I was.

*EXTERIOR: ROAD. DAY.*

MAC (*driving the truck down the road; voice over, singing*):
     See that cloud, there in the sky

*EXTERIOR: MOTEL. DAY.*

MAC (*driving up and parking the truck; voice over, singing*):
     Slowly drifting by
     Well that's the way
     She's adrift from me

     (*He goes to back of house.*)

     Too long I've lied to myself
     I know there's someone else
     But, oh, it hurts so much to face . . .

*INTERIOR: KITCHEN—ROSA LEE'S HOUSE. DAY.*

MAC *comes through the door of kitchen.* SONNY *and* ROSA LEE *are there.*

MAC (*voice over, singing*):
    . . . reality.

    (*To* ROSA LEE:) How you doing?

ROSA LEE: Hi, Mac.

SONNY: You've got a visitor.

MAC (*putting groceries on the table*): Where?

SONNY: In the living room.

MAC (*entering living room*): Yeah?

*INTERIOR: LIVING ROOM. DAY.*

*His daughter,* SUE ANNE, *is there.* MAC *enters.*

SUE ANNE: Do you recognize me?

MAC: Yes, I do.

SUE ANNE: How did you recognize me?

MAC: I just did.

(SONNY *and* ROSA LEE *enter.*)

ROSA LEE: You all excuse us.

(*She leaves with* SONNY. *They go outside.*)

SUE ANNE: You've changed. You don't look like your pictures anymore.

MAC: Don't I? Well, God knows when the last picture of me was taken. It don't make a whole lot of difference about this, but I did try to get in touch with you. I wrote a few letters. Did you ever get them?

SUE ANNE: No.

MAC: Well, your mama didn't have to give them to you. Courts gave her complete jurisdiction. Quite rightly, I guess, considering my state at the time.

SUE ANNE: I told Mama I was coming here. She told me she'd have me arrested if I did. Then Harry reminded her that I'm eighteen now and I don't have to mind anybody. Mama says you tried to kill her once.

MAC: I did.

SUE ANNE: Why did you try to kill her?

MAC: Well, she got me mad some way, I was drunk . . . I don't know. It was one of those things.

SUE ANNE: Someone told Mama the other night you were the best country-western singer they ever heard.

MAC: Oh.

SUE ANNE: Mama threw a glass of whiskey right in her face. She said they were just saying that to spite her. You think you ever will sing again?

MAC: Oh, I think about it once in a while. Sometimes I think I'd like to earn a little money to make things a little easier around here. Or to help out if you ever needed anything.

SUE ANNE: I don't need any money. Mama set up a trust fund for me out of all the royalties she ever earned singing the songs that you wrote. I can buy myself anything I want. Anything I've got has come from your music.

MAC: Well, I'm happy for that. But it wasn't just my music. It was your mama singing it too. Now, you mustn't forget that.

SUE ANNE: I know.

MAC: Yeah . . . Will you have some supper with us?

SUE ANNE: No, thank you. I can't. I have a date tonight. Plays in Mama's band. We have to sneak around 'cause Mama don't like him. Would you like to meet him? He'd like to meet you.

MAC: Oh, I don't think that's such a good idea. I really wouldn't want your mama to think we was ganging up on her behind her back.

SUE ANNE: Well, I could tell her I'm bringing him here.

MAC: Well, all right then.

SUE ANNE: How about tomorrow afternoon?

MAC: Fine.

SUE ANNE: Two o'clock?

MAC: Anytime. I'll be here.

SUE ANNE: You know, you haven't spoken my name once since I've been here. Don't you know my name?

MAC: Sure I know your name. I just kind of been figuring out to myself what I ought to call you. When you were a little girl, I used to call you Sister. I started to call you that this time when I saw you, but I didn't know if it would mean anything to you or not. If you'd remember me doing that.

SUE ANNE: There was a song you used to sing to me when I was little, I think. It was something about a dove. Mama says she never heard you sing it to me. I think it went something about a . . . "On the wings of a snow-white dove, He sends his something, something love."

MAC: I don't remember that, I don't.

(SUE ANNE *walks to door, followed by* MAC.)

*EXTERIOR: MOTEL. DAY.*

ROSA LEE *and* SONNY *walk in the field outside the motel.*

ROSA LEE: So who else had a good science project besides you?

SONNY: Cy Henderson.

(SUE ANNE *comes out of the house and gets in her car.*)

ROSA LEE: Cy did? What did he do?

SONNY: He made this gigantic picture of the world and he showed the crust and the core of the earth. You could open it up.

(ROSA LEE *and* SONNY *stop to watch* SUE ANNE *driving away.*)

*INTERIOR: LIVING ROOM OF ROSA LEE'S HOUSE. DAY.*

MAC *is alone. He walks from door to the window and looks out.*

MAC (*singing*):
> When Jesus went down to the waters that day
> He was baptized in the usual way
> When it was done
> God blessed his soul
> He sent him his love
> On the wings of a dove
> On the wings of a snow-white dove
> He sends his pure, sweet love
> Signs from above
> On the wings of a dove
> On the wings of a dove.

*INTERIOR: GRAPEVINE OPERA HOUSE. NIGHT.*

DIXIE *is on stage singing.*

DIXIE (*singing*):
> I'm still going crazy over you
> I know I'm never getting over you

Over you, I'd gladly be a fool in love again
I know I'm never getting over you.

*INTERIOR: DIXIE'S DRESSING ROOM. NIGHT.*

SUE ANNE *lies on the couch.*

*EXTERIOR: GARAGE IN TOWN. DAY.*

HARRY *and* MAC *walk out of the garage.*

HARRY: Sue Anne's eloped. She left a note. Dixie found it this morning in the hotel. Dixie has gone crazy. Doctor's got her pretty well doped up, but it looks like we're going to have to cancel her show. I don't know what she expects. She spoiled that kid rotten. I tried to tell her a lot of people have been married at eighteen. Some of them even got kids. Dixie was married at eighteen, but I guess you know about that.

MAC: I guess so. Well, what's the boy like she's marrying?

HARRY: No boy. Thirty years old. Been married three times already. Look, if you see her, or if you hear from her, ask her to please call her mama.

MAC: All right, I will.

HARRY: I shouldn't have said what I did about your music.

MAC: It's all right.

(HARRY *takes a check out of his coat pocket. He offers it to* MAC.)

HARRY: I can't promise you nothing, Mac, but I'll take the song with me to Nashville. I'll show it to whoever I can.

MAC (*looking at the check*): What's the five hundred dollars for?

HARRY: It's earnest money, it's good faith money. I owe you that.

MAC: No way, Harry. No Sir.

HARRY: Come on, Mac.

MAC: No Sir. You don't owe me anything. Besides, I've got other plans for the song right now.

HARRY: You got other songs, Mac?

MAC: Yes, I do.

HARRY: You're going to show them to me?

MAC: No.

HARRY: Come on! For Christ's sake!

MAC: No, no. Goddammit, Harry, don't you understand English! I don't want to show them to you.

HARRY: Why?

MAC: Because I don't want to. So stop bugging me.

HARRY: Well, you can't get sore at me for asking you that.

MAC: Let's change the subject, Harry.

HARRY: This is my business. This is my business, for Christ's sake! Look, if you want to do something with your music, you know how to get ahold of me.

MAC: All right.

(HARRY *walks off.*)

*EXTERIOR: MOTEL. DAY.*

MAC *drives up in the truck and gets out and starts towards the motel.*

*INTERIOR: ROSA LEE'S HOUSE. DAY.*

ROSA LEE *is there wiping a mirror.* MAC *enters. He stands in the doorway.*

MAC: You were sixteen when you got married?

ROSA LEE: Yes.

MAC: Dixie was about eighteen when I married her and I was seventeen when I married the first time.

ROSA LEE: You never told me you were married before Dixie.

MAC: No?

ROSA LEE: No.

MAC: I thought I told you everything about me.

ROSA LEE: Well, you didn't tell me that.

MAC: Well, I was trying to get started in the business. (*He comes into the room.*) I was singing in any honky-tonk bar that'd let me through the door. Then I wandered from town to town, city to city, looking for places to sing, finding any kind of work I could in a day to keep me alive so I could sing and play at night. Finally, Lois . . . my first wife's name . . . couldn't stand it and she went home. Then I went back six months later looking for her and I found her living with another man. Said she wanted a divorce, so, hell, I gave it to her. Swore I'd never marry again. Then I met Dixie and changed my mind. And I was making a few records by then and she was singing when I met her and she said she'd give it up when she got married, but then she recorded a song of mine and she done well with it. Said she wanted to sing for five years and get it out of her system. Never happened. Never did. (*Laughs.*) Never did.

(ROSA LEE *walks by* MAC, *briefly resting a hand on his shoulder as she passes.*)

**INTERIOR: CHURCH. DAY.**

ROSA LEE *is again singing in the choir. The* CHOIR DIRECTOR *is conducting as before.*

CHOIR (*singing*):
> When at last I near the shore
> And the fearful breakers roar
> 'Twixt me and the peaceful rest
> Then while he leaned on thy breast
> May I hear thee say to me
> Jesus I will pilot thee.

(*At the front of the church the curtains part.* REVEREND HOTCH-KISS, *with* SONNY *in the baptismal tub, raises his hand.*)

HOTCHKISS: Upon your profession of faith in Our Lord Jesus Christ, I baptize you in the name of the Father and of the Son and of the Holy Spirit.

(HOTCHKISS *takes Sonny's hand and places it over his nose. Then* HOTCHKISS *lays* SONNY *back into the water and lifts him out again. Then* REVEREND HOTCHKISS *draws the curtains closed. Then the curtains at the front of the church part again, revealing* MAC *and* HOTCHKISS *in the baptismal tub.* HOTCHKISS *raises his hand.*)

> Upon your profession of faith in our Lord Jesus Christ, I baptize you in the name of the Father and of the Son and of the Holy Spirit.

FIRST MEMBER OF THE CONGREGATION: Amen.

SECOND MEMBER OF THE CONGREGATION: Amen.

(HOTCHKISS *draws the curtains.*)

*EXTERIOR: ROAD. DAY.*

MAC *drives their truck down the road.* SONNY *and* ROSA LEE *are beside him.*

*INTERIOR: TRUCK. DAY.*

MAC *driving, with* SONNY *and* ROSA LEE *beside him.*

SONNY: Well, we've done it, Mac. We're baptized.

MAC: Yeah, we are.

SONNY: Everybody said I was going to feel like a changed
person. I guess I do feel a little different, but I don't feel a
whole lot different. Do you?

MAC: Not yet.

SONNY: You don't look any different. (*Sits up to look at himself
in the driving mirror.*) Do you think I look any different?

MAC: Not yet.

*EXTERIOR: PLOWBOY'S CLUB. NIGHT.*

*Music sounds from the club, and there are a number of cars and pickup
trucks parked in front.*

*INTERIOR: CLUB. NIGHT.*

*The* SLATER MILL BOYS *are playing. The club is crowded. There
are couples of all ages, some with their children, seated at the table or
dancing.* SONNY *and* ROSA LEE *are seated at a table watching the
dancers and listening to* MAC, *who is on stage singing with the band.*

MAC (*singing*):
> Baby, you're the only dream I've
> Ever had that's come true
> There's so much more to reach for,
> Thanks to you
> All I've heard is me till now

(*Angle: A table near the bandstand. A woman is there with her date.*)

WOMAN (*to her date*): Come on, let's dance. (*She and her date get
up and start dancing.*)

MAC (*singing*):
>   But I see what we've got
>   And if you'll just hold the ladder,
>   Baby, I'll climb to the top
>   If you'll just stand beside me
>   All the way
>   I'll do the things
>   That didn't matter yesterday
>   And I'll be everything this
>   Man can be before I stop
>   If you'll just hold the ladder,
>   Baby, I'll climb to the top
>   Things just started changing
>   With your touch.

(*Angle: A table of four girls.*)

FIRST GIRL (*to others*): I like him.

MAC (*singing*):
>   Yesterday, tomorrow didn't mean as much
>   Now I'll be everything this man
>   Can be before I start
>   If you'll just hold the ladder,
>   Baby, I'll climb to the top
>   If you'll just hold the ladder,
>   Baby, I'll climb to the top.

(MAC *finishes the song. There is applause.* ROSA LEE *and* SONNY *join in the applause.* MAC *gives the microphone to* ROBERT.)

ROBERT: You did it, Mac!

(*The applause continues from the dancers on the floor and the couples still at the tables. The band begins to play again and* MAC *makes his way through the crowd to* ROSA LEE *and* SONNY. *People watch him curiously.*)

WOMAN (*calling out as he passes*): We certainly enjoyed that.

MAN (*calling out*): That was real good, Mac.

(ROSA LEE *and* SONNY *are obviously pleased and proud of him. He joins them at their table.*)

ROSA LEE: That was wonderful.

MAC: Yeah? I was a little nervous.

ROSA LEE: Were you?

MAC: Yeah, a little bit.

ROSA LEE: You couldn't tell. Could you, Sonny?

SONNY: No Ma'am.

MAC: Think I was all right?

ROSA LEE: I thought it was great.

SONNY: I liked it too.

MAC: Mind if your mama and I dance?

SONNY: No Sir.

MAC: Come on, let's go.

(MAC *and* ROSA LEE *leave the table and join the dancers.* SONNY *stays at the table as a* BOY *his age comes up to him.*)

BOY: Is that your daddy?

SONNY: No, that's my step-daddy.

BOY: My mama says he was a famous singer.

SONNY: I guess so. Where's your mama?

BOY (*nodding*): Over there.

(*He points to a* BEARDED MAN *and a* WOMAN *at a nearby table covered with beer bottles.*)

BEARDED MAN (*knocking over bottles*): Ah, Shhee!

(*The* WOMAN *giggles. They are obviously drunk.* SONNY *watches them.*)

SONNY: Is that your daddy with her?

BOY: No, that's a friend of hers. My mom and dad are divorced. Were your mom and dad divorced?

SONNY: No. He died in Vietnam.

BOY: Did he get shot?

SONNY: I guess so.

BOY: Don't you know?

SONNY: No. I don't know how he died.

BOY: Didn't you ever ask?

SONNY: No.

(*The* BEARDED MAN *gets up. He tries to pull the* WOMAN *up.*)

BEARDED MAN (*to* WOMAN): Come on, let's dance, come on.

(*She gets up and they start to dance. The boys watch them.*)

BOY: I hope that man's never my step-daddy.

SONNY: Why, don't you like him?

BOY: No. Do you like your step-daddy?

SONNY: Yes, I do.

BOY: Better than your own daddy?

SONNY: I never knew my own daddy.

BOY: I know mine. He's not so much either.

*INTERIOR: MOTEL OFFICE IN ROSA LEE'S HOUSE. DAY.*

ROSA LEE *is in the office.* SUE ANNE *enters.*

ROSA LEE: Hi.

SUE ANNE: Is my daddy here?

ROSA LEE: Er, no. He's in town. He'll be back in a little while.

SUE ANNE: I wonder if you could cash a check for me?

ROSA LEE: How much?

SUE ANNE: A hundred dollars.

ROSA LEE: Oh, I don't know.

SUE ANNE: Well, the check is good.

ROSA LEE (*opening cash drawer*): Oh, I'm sure of that. I just don't have that much in the cash drawer. I just have twenty-five.

SUE ANNE (*writing check*): Oh, well, that'll help.

(ROSA LEE *takes the money for* SUE ANNE *out of the cash drawer as* SUE ANNE *gives her the check.*)

Appreciate it.

(ROSA LEE *goes into next room.* SUE ANNE *follows her.* ROSA LEE *begins to fold clothes.*)

ROSA LEE: Been back long?

SUE ANNE: Well, we've been back a couple of days.

ROSA LEE: Are you planning to stay around here?

SUE ANNE: I don't know. We may stay, we may move on. My husband has to find work. Mama stopped my trust fund out of spite. (*Pause.*) We met some musicians in Austin the other night that said my daddy just made a new record.

ROSA LEE: Yes, he did.

SUE ANNE: How did it go?

ROSA LEE: Pretty good, I think. He seems pleased.

SUE ANNE: Are you a singer too?

ROSA LEE: I sing with the choir. You know, down at the church.

SUE ANNE: I thought about being a singer, but I don't think I have any voice, to tell you the truth. I guess I was just going on about singing to devil Mama. (*Pause.*) My daddy's quit drinking, they tell me.

ROSA LEE: Yes, he has.

SUE ANNE: How did he quit?

ROSA LEE: I don't know. He just quit.

SUE ANNE: Well, did you ask him to quit?

ROSA LEE: No. He was working here and I told him he couldn't drink while he worked. Sometimes he used to go off and load up, but, gradually, he even stopped that.

SUE ANNE: My husband drinks. Most musicians do, you know. He says he'll quit as soon as he gets work, but . . .

ROSA LEE: Sue Anne, do you have a place to stay?

SUE ANNE: Yes. We're staying at the Jeff Davis Hotel in Austin.

ROSA LEE: Well, if you need a place tomorrow night, you're welcome here.

SUE ANNE: Thank you.

*EXTERIOR: MOTEL. DAY.*

*Sue Anne's car. Her husband is asleep in the car. She gets into the driver's seat and drives off.*

*INTERIOR: DIXIE'S DRESSING ROOM. NIGHT.*

DIXIE: Has anybody in the orchestra heard from them?

HARRY: No.

DIXIE: I give the marriage a month. How long do you give it?

HARRY: I don't know, Dixie.

DIXIE: Don't you at least have an opinion?

HARRY: No. Not about that.

DIXIE: You know what's just come to me?

HARRY: Can't imagine.

DIXIE: Can't imagine?

HARRY: No.

DIXIE: Mac is lying to you.

HARRY: What's he lying to me about?

DIXIE: He knows where they are. He's just not going to tell us out of spite. To spite me. He's trying to get back at us 'cause I wouldn't sing that old song of his.

*EXTERIOR: MOTEL. DAY.*

*The Slater Mill Boys' van drives into the motel blowing its horn. MAC comes out to greet them as they get out of the van. ROBERT hands MAC a copy of their new record. ROSA LEE joins them.*

ROBERT: Here it is, Mac.

HENRY: We just heard it and we're real proud of it.

ROBERT: The record company says it's going to do real good.

HENRY (*pointing to* JAKE): Even Jake here likes it, and not much pleases old Jake.

MAC (*holding record*): I'm glad you boys are pleased.

ROSA LEE: Oh, we'll have to get a record player so that we can listen to it.

ROBERT: You don't have a record player?

ROSA LEE: No. We have a radio and a TV.

ROBERT: Well, you all come over to my house right now and I'll play it for you.

MAC: All right.

ROSA LEE: I'd love to hear it.

MAC: Yeah.

HENRY: We'll see you all over at the house.

MAC: Yes Sir.

ROBERT: Better start listening to the radio too, because they're giving it some play now.

MAC: You bet!

SLATER MILL BOYS (*getting into van and leaving*): See you all soon! See you all later! Bye!

ROSA LEE: Bye!

*INTERIOR: MOTEL OFFICE IN ROSA LEE'S HOUSE. DAY.*

MAC *comes into the room, walks to the table, takes the keys off the hook, and picks up the "will return at" clock sign, then goes back to the door.*

*EXTERIOR: MOTEL. DAY.*

MAC *closes the office door behind him and hangs the "will return" clock on it. The truck radio plays in the background. As MAC adjusts the hands on the clock, the phone rings.*

*INTERIOR: MOTEL OFFICE IN ROSA LEE'S HOUSE.*

MAC *enters to answer the phone. He picks up the receiver.*

MAC (*into phone*): Hello.

*EXTERIOR: MOTEL.*

ROSA LEE *is in the truck turning the dial of the radio.* MAC *comes to the truck and switches the radio off.* MAC *withdraws his hand and walks away as* ROSA LEE *sits puzzled in the driver's seat. He walks up the steps to the porch and sits down on the chair.* ROSA LEE *gets out of the truck and walks up to him.*

MAC: That was Harry Silver. They got a wire this morning that my daughter was killed in an automobile accident, somewhere . . . in northern Louisiana. I didn't catch the name of the town.

*INTERIOR: CAR. DAY.*

MAC *in the back seat.*

MAC (*voice over, singing*):
> A little child, boy or girl
> Will dream and play in their
> Own dream world
> And as they play
> They pretend that they believe
> Well, I'm no child

*EXTERIOR: DIXIE'S HOME. DAY.*

MAC *walks up the steps to the house.* MAC *shakes hand of* MAN *on porch and continues toward the house.*

MAC (*voice over, singing*):
> But at times it's true
> I pretend I'm not losing you
> Because it hurts . . .

*INTERIOR: HALL AND LIVING ROOM OF DIXIE'S HOME.
DAY.*

MAC *enters and* HARRY *shakes hands with him.*

MAC (*voice over, singing*):
   . . . so much to face reality.

HARRY: Dixie's not doing well at all.

MAC: What about Sue Anne's husband?

HARRY: Well, he's going to live. He's in the hospital. He
was—he was drunk.

*INTERIOR: ROOM OFF LIVING ROOM. DAY.*

*Sue Anne's coffin. Her photograph is above the coffin.* MAC *and*
HARRY *enter the room.*

HARRY: It was all his fault. Dixie wanted a closed casket on
account of the accident. I thought it'd be easier on her, on
everybody if we left this down at the funeral parlor, but
she wanted it brought back home.

MAC: Yeah.

(MAC *nods to* HARRY, *who leaves the room, closing the doors behind
him.* MAC *looks at photograph of* SUE ANNE.)

   Little sister.

*INTERIOR: DIXIE'S BEDROOM. DAY.*

DIXIE *is in bed.* HARRY *and* MAC *enter.* HARRY *walks over to
Dixie's bed.*

HARRY: Dixie. Dixie, Mac is here.

DIXIE: Where is he?

HARRY: He's right here.

MAC: Hello, Dixie.

DIXIE: Hello, Mac. Mac . . . why has God done this to me? Why has God done this to me? Oh, you know, I did everything I could to stop her. I . . . I begged and pleaded and I gave her everything in the world she ever wanted. I had nothing when I was her age, do you remember?

MAC: Yeah.

DIXIE: Gave her everything money could . . . (*Crying.*) That was our little girl, Mac. (*She starts out of the bed.*) I want to see my little girl.

(*She takes Harry's hand.* HARRY *tries to keep her in bed.*)

No, I brought her back here to be with me. Please, just let me see her! I want to be with my little girl!

(HARRY *continues trying to restrain her.*)

Let me go, you son-of-a-bitch!

MAC: Be still, be still.

*EXTERIOR: GARDEN NEAR MOTEL. DAY.*

MAC *is weeding the garden rows with a hoe as* ROSA LEE *walks up to him.*

ROSA LEE: Mac, you O.K.?

(*A pause.* MAC *keeps working.*)

MAC: I was almost killed once in a car accident. I was drunk and I ran off the side of the road and I turned over four times. They took me out of that car for dead, but I lived. And I prayed last night to know why I lived and she died, but I got no answer to my prayers. I still don't know why she died and I lived. I don't know the answer to nothing. Not a blessed thing. I don't know why I wandered out to this part of Texas drunk and you took me in and pitied me and helped me to straighten out and married me. Why,

why did this happen? Is there a reason that happened? And Sonny's daddy died in the war. (*Pause.*) My daughter killed in an automobile accident. Why? You see, I don't trust happiness. I never did, I never will.

*EXTERIOR: MOTEL. DAY.*

*School bus drives up and stops.* SONNY *gets off the bus and walks to the motel.*

*INTERIOR: LIVING ROOM—ROSA LEE'S HOUSE. DAY.*

ROSA LEE *is there.* SONNY *comes into the motel.*

SONNY: Where's Mac?

ROSA LEE: He's outside. He got you something. It's in your room.

*INTERIOR: SONNY'S BEDROOM.*

SONNY *enters. He finds a football on his bed. He picks it up and walks away toward the adjoining room.*

*INTERIOR: LIVING ROOM—ROSA LEE'S HOUSE.*

ROSA LEE *is there.* SONNY *enters.*

SONNY: How did my daddy die?

ROSA LEE: I don't know, Sonny.

SONNY: Was he killed in battle?

ROSA LEE: Honey, I just don't know.

SONNY: Well, didn't you ever ask anybody?

ROSA LEE: Yes, I asked someone, and they couldn't tell me anything except that he had been found dead. You see, he was alone when they found him, and they couldn't be sure how long he'd been there, or, if he'd been in a battle, which battle, because there were three in that area that we knew. It could have been in any of them, they said. Or he could have been out walking, they said, and a sniper got him. Where would he be walking to? They didn't have any more idea than I did. He was just a boy, but he was a good boy. I think he would have been a fine man. I think you would have been proud of him. I know he would have been proud of you.

(SONNY *turns and leaves.*)

*EXTERIOR: MOTEL. DAY.*

SONNY *runs down porch steps with the ball.* MAC *is in the garden.*

MAC (*singing, faintly*):
   . . . wings of a snow-white dove
   He sends his pure, sweet love
   Signs from above on the wings . . .
   . . . of a dove
   When Jesus . . .

(SONNY *continues to run.*)

   . . . went down . . .

(MAC *is still gardening as* SONNY *runs toward him.*)

   . . . to the waters that day
   He was baptized in the usual way
   When it was done

SONNY: Thanks for the football, Mac! (*Throws the ball to* MAC.)

MAC: You're welcome, Sonny. (*They begin to pass the football.*) Here's one for you. (*He throws* SONNY *a pass.*) Now throw it to me!

(ROSA LEE *comes out of door to watch as they pass the football to each other. Finally she turns away and returns to the door of the motel.*)

   Come on! Come on! Here you go.

(ROSA LEE *once more looks at the two of them, this time through screen door.* SONNY *laughs as he catches Mac's pass.*)

MAN (*voice over, singing*):
> With tender hands you gathered up
> The pieces of my life,
> Lying in your loving arms
> Never felt so right.
> The hardluck road behind me
> Is reflected in your eyes,
> And the glory of the bright lights
> Can't compare to this feeling
> When you smile.
>
> You're the good things I threw away,
> Coming back to me every day.
> You're the best it could ever be.
> You are what love means to me.
>
> I've been around and seen it all
> From the bottom to the top,
> And honey, I can tell you now,
> I'm thankful for what I've got.
> These prison walls inside me
> Never let this poor soul free,
> Till the power of your true love
> Broke them down just in time
> To rescue me.

MAC: Kick it!

(SONNY *is laughing as he kicks the ball.*)

> Good!

MAN (*voice over, singing*):
> You're the song I could never write.
> You're the magic in my heart tonight.
> When the morning sun comes shining through,
> I'll still be holding you.

You're the good things I threw away,
Coming back to me every day.
You're the best it could ever be.
You are what love means to me.

You're the best it could ever be.
You are what love means to me.

*(The two of them continue to throw the football back and forth until the fade-out.)*

# The Trip to Bountiful

# Cast

|                                          |                   |
| ---------------------------------------- | ----------------- |
| MRS. WATTS                               | Geraldine Page    |
| LUDIE WATTS                              | John Heard        |
| JESSIE MAE                               | Carlin Glynn      |
| SHERIFF                                  | Richard Bradford  |
| THELMA                                   | Rebecca De Mornay |
| ROY, HARRISON TICKET MAN                 | Kevin Cooney      |
| ROSELLA                                  | Mary Kay Mars     |
| TICKET MAN #1                            | Norman Bennett    |
| TICKET MAN #2                            | Harvey Lewis      |
| TICKET AGENT, HOUSTON TRAIN STATION      | Kirk Sisco        |
| BILLY DAVIS                              | Dave Tanner       |
| BUS ATTENDANT GERARD                     | Gil Glasgow       |
| BUS OPERATOR                             | Jerry Nelson      |
| BLACK WOMAN ON BUS                       | Wezz Tildon       |
| DOWNSTAIRS NEIGHBOR                      | Peggy Ann Byers   |
| MEXICAN MAN                              | David Romo        |

# Credits

Produced by Sterling VanWagenen
Directed by Peter Masterson
Screenplay by Horton Foote,
based on his play *The Trip to Bountiful*
Director of Photography: Fred Murphy
Music by J.A.C. Redford
Art Director: Philip Lamb
Film Editor: Jay Freund
Costumes by Gary Jones


A Filmdallas I and Bountiful Film Partners Production
Distributed by Island Pictures

*FADE IN.*
*A field of bluebonnets in the Texas countryside. A young boy is seen running through the bluebonnets, followed by his mother, who is also running.*

WOMAN (*voice over, singing*):
>Softly and tenderly Jesus is calling,
>Calling for you and for me;
>See, on the portals he's waiting and watching,
>Watching for you and for me.
>Come home, come home,
>Ye who are weary, come home;
>Earnestly, tenderly, Jesus is calling,
>Calling, O sinner, come home.

*INTERIOR: THE FRONT ROOM OF THE WATTS' HOUSTON APARTMENT. NIGHT.*

MRS. CARRIE WATTS *is seated in a rocking chair looking out the window and humming quietly to herself the hymn that has just been heard.*

*INTERIOR: BEDROOM—WATTS' APARTMENT.*

LUDIE *and his wife,* JESSIE MAE, *are in single beds.* JESSIE MAE *is sound asleep, but* LUDIE *is awake and after a moment starts out of the bed.*

*INTERIOR: FRONT ROOM.*

MRS. WATTS *continues rocking and humming the hymn.* LUDIE *comes in; he has a book in his hand. He opens the book as he stands near the bedroom door and begins to read.*

MRS. WATTS: Don't try to be quiet, Sonny. I'm awake.

LUDIE: Yes Ma'am.

MRS. WATTS: Couldn't you sleep?

LUDIE: No Ma'am.

MRS. WATTS: Why couldn't you sleep?

LUDIE: Just couldn't. Couldn't you sleep?

MRS. WATTS: No, I haven't been to bed at all. You're not worrying about your job, are you, Sonny?

LUDIE: No Ma'am. Everybody seems to like me there. (*He closes the book and puts it on a table.*) I'm thinking about asking for a raise.

MRS. WATTS: Oh, you should, hard as you work.

LUDIE (*going to the couch and sitting*): Why couldn't you sleep, Mama?

MRS. WATTS (*going to the window and looking out*): Because of the full moon. I never could sleep when there was a full moon. Even back in Bountiful when I'd been working out in the fields all day, and I'd be so tired I'd think my legs would give out on me, let there be a full moon and I'd just toss the night away. (*Goes to* LUDIE.) I remember once when you were little and there was a full moon, I woke you up and dressed you and took you for a walk with me. Do you remember?

LUDIE: No Ma'am.

MRS. WATTS: You don't?

LUDIE: No Ma'am.

MRS. WATTS: Well, I remember just like it was yesterday. I dressed you and took you outside. And there was an old dog howling away someplace and that scared you. I just held you and you were trembling with fear. And you said someone had told you that when a dog howled a person was dying somewhere. And I held you close to me, and then you asked me to explain to you about dying. And I said you were too young to worry about things like that for a long time to come.

LUDIE: Funny the things you think of when you can't sleep. I was trying to think of the song I used to like to hear you sing.

MRS. WATTS: Oh, what was that, Sonny?

LUDIE: I don't remember the name. I just remember I'd always laugh when you'd sing it.

*INTERIOR: BEDROOM.*

JESSIE MAE *stirs in her sleep.*

MRS. WATTS (*off camera*): Oh, that old song? How'd it go? Just hate it when I can't think of things.

*INTERIOR: FRONT ROOM.*

MRS. WATTS *is still trying to recall the song.*

MRS. WATTS:
> Hush little baby, don't say a word
> Mama's gonna buy you a mockingbird.

(*She begins to half-sing it.*)

> And if that mockingbird don't sing,
> Mama's gonna buy you a diamond ring.

(*She and* LUDIE *laugh as she finishes. Pause.*)

I used to think I was gonna buy you the world back in those days. I remember remarking that to my papa. He said the world can't be bought. I didn't really understand what he meant by that then. Ludie . . . would you like me to get you some hot milk?

LUDIE: Yes Ma'am. If you don't mind.

(MRS. WATTS *goes to the kitchen.*)

*INTERIOR: KITCHEN.*

A *small efficiency kitchen, once part of the front room. There is a window over the stove that allows a view of the front room.* MRS. WATTS *gets milk and begins to heat it. She sees* JESSIE MAE *come into the front room and turn on the lights.*

JESSIE MAE: How do you expect to work tomorrow if you don't get your sleep, Ludie?

(JESSIE MAE *turns on the radio.* MRS. WATTS *brings the hot milk to* LUDIE. *He begins to drink it.*)

Mother Watts, where did you put that recipe that Rosella gave me on the phone today?

MRS. WATTS: Jessie Mae, I don't remember you having given me any recipe.

JESSIE MAE: Well, I did. This morning, right here in this very room, and I asked you to please put it on my dresser and you said I will and went out holding it in your hand.

MRS. WATTS: Did you look on your dresser?

JESSIE MAE: Yes Ma'am.

MRS. WATTS: And it wasn't there?

JESSIE MAE: No Ma'am. I looked just before I went to bed.

(MRS. WATTS *goes back into kitchen.*)

> We're just gonna have to get out a little more, Ludie. It's no wonder you can't sleep. Every couple I know goes out three or four times a week.

*INTERIOR: KITCHEN.*

MRS. WATTS *is looking for the recipe.*

JESSIE MAE (*off camera*): I know we couldn't afford it before, so I kept quiet about it.

*INTERIOR: FRONT ROOM.*

JESSIE MAE: And now you're working again I don't think a picture show once or twice a week would break us.

LUDIE: Okay, why don't we go out one night this week?

*INTERIOR: KITCHEN.*

MRS. WATTS *continues her search for the recipe.*

JESSIE MAE (*off camera*): Well, I mean, I think we have to. I was talking to Rosella about it this morning on the phone.

*INTERIOR: FRONT ROOM.*

LUDIE: When did you and Rosella get friendly again?

JESSIE MAE: This morning. She just all of a sudden called me up on the telephone. She said she would quit being mad if I would.

*INTERIOR: KITCHEN.*

MRS. WATTS *continues to search for recipe.*

JESSIE MAE (*off camera*): I said, shucks, she was the one that was mad. I told her I was plainspoken and said exactly what I felt and people will just have to take me as I am or just leave me alone.

*INTERIOR: FRONT ROOM.*

LUDIE *takes his book and begins reading again.*

JESSIE MAE: Rosella found out definitely that she can't have any children . . .

(MRS. WATTS *comes hurrying back into the front room.*)

　　　　(*To* MRS. WATTS:) Walk, don't run.

*INTERIOR: LUDIE AND JESSIE MAE'S BEDROOM.*

*From the front room,* MRS. WATTS *is seen as she enters Ludie and Jessie Mae's bedroom and begins to search for the recipe.*

*INTERIOR: FRONT ROOM.*

JESSIE MAE: Your mother's pension check didn't come today. It's the eighteenth. I swear it was due. I just don't understand the government. Always late.

*INTERIOR: BEDROOM.*

MRS. WATTS *is at a chest of drawers looking for the recipe.*

*INTERIOR: FRONT ROOM.*

JESSIE MAE: Rosella was glad to hear you're working again. She said she was cleaning out some drawers night before last and come across some pictures she had taken of you and me when we started going together. I said I don't care to see them. No, thank you. The passing of time makes me sad.

MRS. WATTS (*coming into the front room with the recipe*): Here's your recipe.

JESSIE MAE: Thank you. Where did you find it?

MRS. WATTS: In your room.

JESSIE MAE: In my room?

MRS. WATTS: Yes Ma'am.

JESSIE MAE: Where in my room?

MRS. WATTS: In your dresser drawer. Right-hand side.

JESSIE MAE: In my dresser drawer?

MRS. WATTS: I looked on top of the dresser and it wasn't there and something said to me . . .

JESSIE MAE: Mother Watts!

MRS. WATTS: Ma'am?

JESSIE MAE: Ludie. How many times have I asked her never to look into my dresser drawers?

MRS. WATTS: I thought you wanted me to . . .

JESSIE MAE (*interrupting*): I did not want you to go into my dresser drawers. I'd like a little privacy if you don't mind.

MRS. WATTS: Yes Ma'am.

JESSIE MAE: And don't you ever let me catch you looking in them again. For anything. I can't stand people snooping in my dresser drawers.

MRS. WATTS (*grabbing the recipe out of Jessie Mae's hand and throwing it on the floor*): Then the next time you find it yourself.

JESSIE MAE: You pick that recipe up, if you please!

MRS. WATTS: Pick it up yourself. I have no intention of picking it up.

JESSIE MAE: You pick that up!

MRS. WATTS: I won't!

LUDIE: Mama.

JESSIE MAE: You will!

LUDIE: Jessie Mae. For God sakes! You're both acting like children. It's one-thirty in the morning.

JESSIE MAE: You make her pick that up.

MRS. WATTS: I won't.

JESSIE MAE: You will! This is my house and you'll do exactly as you're told.

(LUDIE *goes into the bedroom.*)

I hope you're satisfied. You've got Ludie good and upset. He won't sleep for the rest of the night. What do you want to do? Get him sick again?

MALE NEIGHBOR'S VOICE (*off camera*): Shut that goddamn radio off!

JESSIE MAE (*yelling up to neighbor*): Shut up. (*To* MRS. WATTS:) Oh, you're going too far with me one of these days, old lady.

LUDIE (*coming back in*): Jessie Mae.

JESSIE MAE: I can't stand this, Ludie. I'm at the end of my rope. I won't take being insulted by your mother or anyone else. You hear that?

(JESSIE MAE *goes into the bedroom.* MRS. WATTS *picks up the recipe and hands it to* LUDIE.)

LUDIE: Mama, will you give this recipe to Jessie Mae?

MRS. WATTS: All right, Sonny.

LUDIE: Mama, will you please tell Jessie Mae you're sorry?

MRS. WATTS: Ludie . . .

LUDIE: Please, Mama.

MRS. WATTS: All right, Ludie.

*INTERIOR: BEDROOM.*

JESSIE MAE *is at her dressing table, her back to the door.* MRS. WATTS *enters, and* JESSIE MAE *pays no attention.* LUDIE *stands in the door watching.*

LUDIE: Jessie Mae.

JESSIE MAE: What do you want, Ludie?

LUDIE: Mama has something to say to you.

JESSIE MAE: What is it?

(MRS. WATTS *hands her the recipe.* JESSIE MAE *turns and looks at her.*)

MRS. WATTS: Jessie Mae, I'm sorry for throwing the recipe on the floor. (*Hands the recipe to* JESSIE MAE.)

JESSIE MAE: I accept your apology.

(MRS. WATTS *goes to the front room.*)

LUDIE: Jessie Mae. I know it's hard and all, but for your own sake I sometimes think if you'd try to ignore certain things . . .

JESSIE MAE: Ignore? How can you ignore something when it's done right under your very nose?

LUDIE: Jessie Mae . . .

JESSIE MAE: I know her, Ludie. She does things just to aggravate me.

*INTERIOR: FRONT ROOM.*

MRS. WATTS *is in her rocking chair.*

JESSIE MAE (*off camera*): Now you take her hymn singing. She never starts until I come into a room. And her pouting!

*INTERIOR: BEDROOM.*

JESSIE MAE: Why sometimes she goes a whole day just sitting and staring out that window. How would you like to spend twenty-four hours a day shut up with a woman that either sang hymns or looked out the window and pouted?

LUDIE: I'm not saying it's easy, Jessie Mae . . .

JESSIE MAE: She just keeps me so nervous. Never knowing when I leave whether she is going to try to run off to that old town or not.

*INTERIOR: FRONT ROOM.*

MRS. WATTS *gets out of her chair.*

LUDIE (*off camera*): She's not going to run off again, Jessie Mae. She promised she wouldn't.

(MRS. WATTS *goes to the edge of the rug, lifts it up, and takes out the pension check.*)

JESSIE MAE (*off camera*): Sometimes I think she hides that check, and I tell you right now if it is not here tomorrow I am going to search the house from top to bottom.

(MRS. WATTS *puts the check inside her nightgown and then goes back to her rocking chair.*)

Rosella asked me if I realized that it would be fifteen years this August since we were married. I will never forget the night I came home and told Rosella that you had proposed.

*INTERIOR: BEDROOM.*

JESSIE MAE: I thought you were the handsomest man alive.

LUDIE: And I thought you were the prettiest girl.

JESSIE MAE: Did you, Ludie?

LUDIE: Jessie Mae, I've got to start making some more money. I'm thinking about asking for a raise. I'm entitled to it. I've been there six months now. I haven't been late or sick once. I'm gonna walk into Mr. Douglas' office the first thing in the morning and I'm going to say, Mr. Douglas, I've got to have a raise starting as of now. We can't live on what you pay us.

JESSIE MAE: Well . . . I would.

LUDIE: I don't understand it, Jessie Mae. I try not to be bitter. I try not to . . .

*INTERIOR: FRONT ROOM.*

MRS. WATTS *is in her chair. She can hear snatches of their conversation.*

LUDIE (*off camera*): I don't know. All I know is that a man works with a company for eight years . . . He saves a little money. He gets sick and has to spend two years in bed watching his savings all go. Then start all over with a new company.

*INTERIOR: BEDROOM.*

LUDIE: Of course, the doctor says I shouldn't worry about it. He says I've got to take things like they come. That's what I try to do. Every day.

JESSIE MAE: What's this book?

LUDIE: It's mine. I bought it at the drugstore coming from the office.

JESSIE MAE (*reading*): "How to Become an Executive."

LUDIE: My boss likes me. Billy Davis told me he was positive he did. Billy Davis has been there ten years now, you know. Feeling sleepy now?

JESSIE MAE: Yes. Are you?

LUDIE: Yes, I am. Good night.

JESSIE MAE: Good night.

*INTERIOR: FRONT ROOM.*

MRS. WATTS *is there.* LUDIE *enters. She looks around at him.*

MRS. WATTS: I'm all right, Sonny. I'm just still not sleepy.

LUDIE (*turning off the radio and going to his mother*): Good night. (*He kisses her.*)

MRS. WATTS: Ludie, please, Son, I want to go home.

LUDIE: Mama, you know I can't make a living there. We have to live in Houston.

MRS. WATTS: Son, Ludie. I can't stay here any longer. I want to go home.

LUDIE: I beg you not to ask me this again. There's nothing I can do about it. (*Goes out.*)

*EXTERIOR: APARTMENT—HOUSTON. NEXT MORNING.*

*A woman walks a dog. Early morning traffic has begun.*

*INTERIOR: FRONT ROOM. MORNING.*

MRS. WATTS *awakes with a start and looks for the check inside her nightgown. She finds it and hides it under the mattress of the couch. She then goes toward the kitchen.*

MRS. WATTS (*calling*): Ludie, it's eight-fifteen. Ludie, Ludie.

*INTERIOR: KITCHEN.*

MRS. WATTS *enters.*

MRS. WATTS: It's eight-fifteen.

*INTERIOR: BATHROOM.*

LUDIE *is shaving.*

LUDIE: Yes'm.

*INTERIOR: KITCHEN.*

MRS. WATTS *is making coffee and singing* "We Shall Gather at the River."

*INTERIOR: BEDROOM.*

JESSIE MAE *is getting out of bed.*

JESSIE MAE: It's too early for hymn singing.

*INTERIOR: KITCHEN.*

MRS. WATTS *is filling two cups with coffee.*

*INTERIOR: FRONT ROOM.*

JESSIE MAE *appears in doorway as* MRS. WATTS *hurries out of the kitchen with the two cups of coffee.*

JESSIE MAE: Walk, don't run.

(MRS. WATTS *takes the coffee to a table and goes back to the kitchen.* JESSIE MAE *turns on the radio.*)

*INTERIOR: BEDROOM.*

LUDIE *is knotting his tie.*

*INTERIOR: KITCHEN.*

MRS. WATTS *is making toast.* LUDIE *comes into the front room.*

LUDIE: Good morning, Mama.

MRS. WATTS: Good morning, Son. I'll have your toast ready
    for you in a minute.

(JESSIE MAE *and* LUDIE *go to the table and begin to drink their coffee.*)

LUDIE: Why don't we have an early supper tonight? Six-thirty, if that's all right with you and Mama. And after supper I'll take you both to the picture show.

(MRS. WATTS *brings their toast to them and goes into bedroom.*)

JESSIE MAE: Do you want to go downtown or one of the neighborhood movies?

LUDIE: Whatever you want to do.

JESSIE MAE: Maybe it would do us good to go downtown.

LUDIE: Billy's picking me up. I want to get in early. Mr. Douglas is usually in before nine. I think I'm doing the right thing, asking for a raise. Don't you?

JESSIE MAE: Sure. (*Goes to the phone.*) Oh, Rita. This is Jessie Mae Watts. Can I have an appointment for my hair? Two o'clock.

*INTERIOR: BEDROOM.*

MRS. WATTS *is making the beds. She is listening to Jessie Mae's conversation. She can see into the front room as she works. She sees* LUDIE *kiss* JESSIE MAE *goodbye.*

JESSIE MAE: Nothing earlier? See you then.

LUDIE: Goodbye, Mama.

MRS. WATTS: Goodbye, Son.

JESSIE MAE: Holler if there's any mail down there.

LUDIE: I will.

*EXTERIOR: APARTMENT.*

*Billy Davis' car is waiting.* LUDIE *comes out.*

LUDIE: No mail for us.

*EXTERIOR: BALCONY OF WATTS' APARTMENT.*

JESSIE MAE *is there.*

JESSIE MAE: All right.

(*She watches* LUDIE *get in the car and the car drive off.*)

*INTERIOR: FRONT ROOM.*

JESSIE MAE *enters.*

JESSIE MAE: I can't understand about that pension check, can you?

*INTERIOR: BEDROOM.*

MRS. WATTS *is still making the beds.*

MRS. WATTS: No Ma'am.

JESSIE MAE (*off camera*): You know, you're so absentminded. You don't think you put it around the room someplace by mistake.

MRS. WATTS: I don't believe so.

*INTERIOR: FRONT ROOM.*

JESSIE MAE *takes Mrs. Watts' purse off the wardrobe and looks inside. She finds nothing and closes it and puts it back.*

*INTERIOR: BEDROOM.*

MRS. WATTS *continues working in the bedroom.*

*INTERIOR: FRONT ROOM.*

JESSIE MAE *looks around room.*

*INTERIOR: BEDROOM.*

MRS. WATTS *continues working.* JESSIE MAE *comes in and goes to*

*her clothes closet and takes out dresses and tries to decide what to wear.*
MRS. WATTS *passes her on the way to the front room.*

*INTERIOR: BATHROOM.*

JESSIE MAE *comes into the bathroom.*

*INTERIOR: FRONT ROOM.*

MRS. WATTS *hears* JESSÌE MAE *go into the bathroom. She takes the
check from the couch and puts it inside her dress.*

*INTERIOR: BILLY DAVIS' CAR.*

BILLY DAVIS *and* LUDIE *are inside.*

BILLY DAVIS: Bus wasn't fast enough for you this morning,
huh, Ludie?

LUDIE: No, I was hoping to get a chance to speak to the boss
before we started our work this morning. How is everything with your family?

BILLY DAVIS: Oh, fine. The children were full of life this
morning, as usual. I said to Myrtle Sue, "My Lord have
mercy, we have a lot of live wires around here, don't we?"
How is your wife?

LUDIE: She's fine.

BILLY DAVIS: Your mother lives with you, too, doesn't she?

LUDIE: Yes, she does.

*INTERIOR: FRONT ROOM.*

JESSIE MAE *is there.* MRS. WATTS *enters.*

JESSIE MAE: I'm going to call Rosella and tell her to meet me
at the drugstore for a Coke.

(MRS. WATTS *is humming to herself.*)

Will you stop that hymn singing? Do you want me to jump right out of my skin? You know what hymns do to my nerves.

(MRS. WATTS *stops humming and sits in a chair.*)

And don't pout. You know I can't stand pouting. (*Goes to the phone and dials.*)

MRS. WATTS: I didn't mean to pout, Jessie Mae. I only meant to be silent.

JESSIE MAE (*hanging up phone*): She's not home. I bet she's at the drugstore right now.

(MRS. WATTS *has a vacuum cleaner and is sweeping around the room.*)

I can't make up my mind what movie I want to see tonight. Well, I'll ask Rosella. Will you stop that noise for a minute? I'm nervous.

(MRS. WATTS *stops vacuuming.*)

You know, when I first came to Houston I went to three picture shows in one day. I went to the Kirby in the morning, and the Metropolitan in the afternoon, and the Majestic that night.

(MRS. WATTS *is getting physically weaker. She sways and reaches for the sofa to keep from falling.*)

Mother Watts . . .

MRS. WATTS: I'm all right, Jessie Mae.

JESSIE MAE: Is it your heart?

MRS. WATTS: It's . . . a little sinking spell. Just let me lie down on the sofa for a minute and I'll be all right. (*Lies down on the sofa.*)

JESSIE MAE: Can I get you some water?

MRS. WATTS: Thank you.

(JESSIE MAE *runs into the kitchen for the water.*)

JESSIE MAE (*off camera*): Do you want me to call Ludie?

MRS. WATTS: No Ma'am.

(JESSIE MAE *comes back with the glass of water.* MRS. WATTS *drinks it.*)

JESSIE MAE: Are you feeling better now?

MRS. WATTS: Yes, I am, Jessie Mae. (*Gets up off the sofa.*)

JESSIE MAE: Do you think you ought to get up so soon?

MRS. WATTS: I'm feeling much better already. (*Walks over to a chair.*) I'll just sit here in the chair.

JESSIE MAE: All right. I'll just sit here for a while and keep you company. (*Sits in a chair near* MRS. WATTS.) It always scares the daylights out of me when you get one of those sinking spells.

*EXTERIOR: PARKING LOT.*

BILLY DAVIS *drives up and parks his car. He and* LUDIE *get out and walk toward their workplace.*

LUDIE: Well, what do you think about the Buffs' chances for the Dixie Series?

BILLY DAVIS: They're gonna have to win the Texas League first.

LUDIE: That's right.

BILLY DAVIS: Myrtle Sue and I are going to Buff Stadium Friday night. If you'd like to go . . .

*INTERIOR: FRONT ROOM.*

MRS. WATTS *is still resting.* JESSIE MAE *waits with her. The phone rings, and* JESSIE MAE *answers.*

JESSIE MAE: Oh, hello, Rosella, I tried to call you earlier. Oh. You're at the drugstore. That's what I just figured. Well, I'd like to, Rosella, but Mother Watts has had a sinking spell . . .

MRS. WATTS: Oh no . . . you go on, Jessie Mae. I'm going to be all right. I'll just rest here. There's nothing you can do for me.

JESSIE MAE: Are you sure?

MRS. WATTS: I'm sure, Jessie Mae.

JESSIE MAE: Well, all right, then. (*Into phone:*) Rosella, Mother Watts says she won't need me here. So I think I will come over for a while. All right. I'll see you then. Bye. (*To* MRS. WATTS:) Are you sure you'll be all right?

MRS. WATTS: Oh, yes, Jessie Mae.

JESSIE MAE: Well, I'll go on over then. Now, you call me at the drugstore if you need me. You hear?

MRS. WATTS: Oh, yes Ma'am.

*EXTERIOR: APARTMENT HOUSE.*

JESSIE MAE *comes out of the house.*

*INTERIOR: FRONT ROOM.*

MRS. WATTS *is at window watching* JESSIE MAE *go down the street.* MRS. WATTS *then takes the check and starts to endorse it as* JESSIE MAE *comes back into the room.*

JESSIE MAE: I forgot to take any money.

(*She goes into the bedroom without looking at* MRS. WATTS. *As soon as she is out of the room* MRS. WATTS *runs to shelf and gets writing paper and brings it back to where she was endorsing the check, puts the check inside her dress, and starts to write a letter.* JESSIE MAE *comes back in.*)

Who are you writing to?

MRS. WATTS: I just thought I'd drop a line to Callie Davis and let her know I'm still alive.

JESSIE MAE: Why did you decide to do that all of a sudden?

MRS. WATTS: No reason. The notion just struck me.

JESSIE MAE: All right. (*Starts out.*) But just in case you're trying to put something over on me with that pension check, I've told Mr. Reynolds at the grocery store never to cash anything for you.

(JESSIE MAE *leaves.* MRS. WATTS *goes to window and looks out. Again she sees* JESSIE MAE *walking down the street. She runs to the bureau, opens a drawer, and takes out some clothes. She gets a small suitcase from under the couch, puts the clothes in the suitcase, goes back to the dresser and looks at some family pictures on top of the dresser, selects a few to take with her, puts them in the suitcase, and closes it. Then she takes her hat and a coat, picks up the suitcase, and goes hurrying out.*)

*INTERIOR: APARTMENT—STAIRS.*

MRS. WATTS *hurries down the stairs.*

*EXTERIOR: APARTMENT.*

MRS. WATTS *comes out of the door leading to her apartment as her downstairs neighbor comes out of her front door.*

WOMAN NEIGHBOR: Morning, Mrs. Watts.

MRS. WATTS: Good morning. How you doing?

WOMAN NEIGHBOR: Just fine.

*EXTERIOR: STREET.*

MRS. WATTS *hurries down the street.*

*EXTERIOR: DRUGSTORE.*

JESSIE MAE *comes by drugstore. She can see* ROSELLA *through drugstore window. They wave to each other.* JESSIE MAE *goes into drugstore.*

*EXTERIOR: STREET.*

MRS. WATTS *hurries down the street to the bus stop. She sits on the bench at the bus stop.*

*INTERIOR: DRUGSTORE.*

ROSELLA *and* JESSIE MAE *are finishing their Coca-Colas.* JESSIE MAE *looks up at the drugstore clock.*

JESSIE MAE: Oh, child . . . look at that clock. It's ten-fifteen. Maybe I'd better get back up to Mother Watts. She wasn't feeling so well this morning.

*INTERIOR: DRESS SHOP.*

ROSELLA *and* JESSIE MAE *are looking at dresses.*

*EXTERIOR: BUS STOP.*

*A bus pulls up.* MRS. WATTS *gets on the bus.*

*INTERIOR: TRAIN STATION.*

MRS. WATTS *enters. She goes up to the ticket agent.*

MRS. WATTS: Ticket to Bountiful, please?

TICKET AGENT: Where?

MRS. WATTS: Bountiful. It's between Harrison and Cotton.

TICKET AGENT: No trains to there anymore.

MRS. WATTS: Are you sure?

TICKET AGENT: Yes, I'm sure.

MRS. WATTS: Well, there used to be excursions between Bountiful and Houston, you know. I remember because I've . . .

TICKET AGENT (*interrupting*): No trains go there now.

*EXTERIOR: CITY STREET.*

MRS. WATTS *hurries down the street.*

*INTERIOR: BUS STATION.*

MRS. WATTS *comes in and stands in the ticket line.*

*INTERIOR: APARTMENT.*

JESSIE MAE *enters the front room.*

JESSIE MAE (*calling*): Mother Watts, I'm home. Mother Watts?

*INTERIOR: TICKET COUNTER—BUS STATION.*

MRS. WATTS *is so busy watching the doors that she doesn't notice it's her turn.*

BUS TICKET MAN: Lady . . . lady, it's your turn.

MRS. WATTS: Oh, yes. Excuse me. I'd like a ticket to Bountiful, please.

BUS TICKET MAN: Where?

MRS. WATTS: To Bountiful.

BUS TICKET MAN: What's it near?

MRS. WATTS: It's between Harrison and Cotton.

BUS TICKET MAN: I can sell you a ticket to Harrison or to Cotton. But there's no Bountiful.

MRS. WATTS: Oh, yes there is. It's between Harrison and . . .

BUS TICKET MAN: I'm sorry, lady. You say there is, but the book says there isn't. And the book don't lie.

MRS. WATTS: But I . . .

BUS TICKET MAN: Make up your mind, lady. Cotton or Harrison. There are other people waiting.

MRS. WATTS: How much is a ticket to Harrison?

BUS TICKET MAN: Three-fifty.

MRS. WATTS: Cotton?

BUS TICKET MAN: Four-twenty.

MRS. WATTS: Give me a ticket to Harrison, please.

BUS TICKET MAN: That'll be three-fifty, please.

MRS. WATTS: Yessir. (*Reaches for her pocketbook and is about to open it. She turns to the* TICKET MAN.) Could you cash a pension check? You see I decided to come at the last minute and didn't have time to stop by the . . .

BUS TICKET MAN: Can't cash any checks.

MRS. WATTS: It's perfectly good. It's a government check.

BUS TICKET MAN: I'm sorry. Makes no difference. It's against the rules to cash checks.

MRS. WATTS: Oh, is that so? I understand that. A rule's a rule. How much was that again?

BUS TICKET MAN: Three-fifty.

MRS. WATTS: Oh yes . . . three . . . Just a minute.

(*She opens her purse and takes out two dollar bills and puts them on the counter. Then she reaches in her pocket and takes out some silver tied up in a handkerchief.*)

It's all here in nickels and dimes and quarters.

(*She unties the handkerchief and places it on the counter and begins to count the silver.*)

I believe that is three-fifty.

BUS TICKET MAN: Thank you. (*Rakes the money into his hand.*)

MRS. WATTS: That's quite all right. Sorry to have taken up so much of your time. (*Picks up her suitcase and starts off.*)

BUS TICKET MAN: Here lady. Don't forget your ticket.

(*She comes running back.*)

MRS. WATTS: Oh, good heavens. I'd forget my head if it wasn't on my neck.

(MRS. WATTS *takes the ticket and goes to a bench where* THELMA *is seated, reading. She sits with her back to* THELMA, *looks around and* THELMA *sees her.*)

THELMA: Good afternoon.

MRS. WATTS: Good afternoon. Would you watch my suit-case, honey? I'll be right back.

(*She takes her suitcase and puts it beside* THELMA. MRS. WATTS *goes running toward the door to the street. She looks out for a moment and then goes back to* THELMA.)

Is this seat taken?

THELMA: No.

MRS. WATTS (*sitting beside* THELMA): A little warm, isn't it, when you're running around.

THELMA: Yes'm.

MRS. WATTS: I had to get myself ready in the biggest kind of hurry. And I'm trying to get to a town nobody around here heard of.

THELMA: What town is that?

MRS. WATTS: Bountiful.

THELMA: Oh.

MRS. WATTS: Did you ever hear of it?

THELMA: No.

MRS. WATTS: You know, that's what I mean. Nobody heard of it. Not much of a town left, I guess. I haven't seen it myself, what was it, in twenty years. It used to be quite prosperous. All they have left is a post office and a . . . a filling station and a general store. At least when I left it.

THELMA: Do your people live there?

MRS. WATTS: No. My people are all dead. Except my son and his wife, Jessie Mae. They live here in the city. I'm hurrying to see Bountiful before I die. I had a sinking spell this morning. I had to climb up on the bed and rest. It was my heart.

THELMA: Do you have a bad heart?

MRS. WATTS: Well, it's not what you call a good one. Doctor says it would last me as long as I need it if I could just cut out worrying. But seems I can't do that lately. (*Gets up.*) Would you keep your eye on that suitcase again?

THELMA: Yes Ma'am.

(MRS. WATTS *hurries over to the window and peers out at the street.*)

　　Is there anything wrong?

MRS. WATTS: No, honey. I'm just a little nervous. That's all.

(*The city bus stops outside the window behind* MRS. WATTS. LUDIE *and* JESSIE MAE *get off the bus and start into the station.* MRS. WATTS *turns and sees them just outside the window.* MRS. WATTS

*runs over to the seat and picks up the suitcase, leaving her hand-
kerchief in the seat.*)

Say a prayer for me, honey. Good luck.

THELMA: Good luck to you.

(MRS. WATTS *goes running off as* LUDIE *and* JESSIE MAE *come
into the bus station.* LUDIE *looks around.* JESSIE MAE *follows after
him.*)

JESSIE MAE: Ludie, she always tries to go by train. But no.
We wait at one railroad station five minutes, and because
she isn't there right then, you drag me over here. We've
always found her there. Why, she won't believe them at
the depot if they tell her there's not a train to Bountiful.
She says there is and you watch, as far as she's concerned
that's how it'll have to be.

*INTERIOR: BUS STATION CAFE.*

LUDIE *goes into cafe,* JESSIE MAE *following.*

JESSIE MAE: I think we ought to just turn this whole thing
over to the police. That would scare her once and for all.

LUDIE: We're not going to call any police.

*INTERIOR: BUS STATION WAITING ROOM.*

LUDIE *and* JESSIE MAE *enter.* LUDIE *runs over to the ticket
window.*

LUDIE: Did a lady come here and buy a ticket to a town
named Bountiful?

SECOND BUS TICKET MAN: Not since I've been on duty.

LUDIE: How long have you been on duty?

SECOND BUS TICKET MAN: About fifteen minutes.

(LUDIE *goes toward magazine stand.* JESSIE MAE *sits next to* THELMA. THELMA *is reading.*)

JESSIE MAE (*to* THELMA): Excuse me. Do you have a match? My lighter's out of fluid.

(THELMA *finds a book of matches and gives them to her.*)

Thank you. I hope you're lucky enough not to have to fool with any in-laws. I've got a mother-in-law about to drive me crazy. She's always trying to run off to this place called Bountiful. Of course, there hasn't been a train to that town in I don't know when. But if you try to tell her that, she just looks at you like you're making it up. But I was too trusting today. I gave her every chance in the world to get away. People ask me why I don't have any children. I say I've got Ludie and Mother Watts. That's all the children I need.

(LUDIE *comes in with a movie magazine. He comes up to* JESSIE MAE.)

(*To* LUDIE:) What did you bring me? (*Looks at the magazine.*) Oh, I've seen that one. I think we're wasting our time sitting here.

LUDIE: Do you want to go to the other train station?

JESSIE MAE: I don't care what you do. It's your mother.

(JESSIE MAE *walks away.* LUDIE *goes to* THELMA.)

LUDIE: Would you like this? I never read them and my wife has seen it.

THELMA: Thank you.

(THELMA *takes the magazine.* LUDIE *looks at the bench and sees the handkerchief that was dropped by* MRS. WATTS. *He takes it and goes running over to the magazine counter.*)

LUDIE (*to* MAGAZINE MAN): Pardon, do you suppose you've
seen a woman about. . . . Oh . . .

(*He sees* THELMA *get up to leave the terminal. He goes to her.*)

Excuse me, Miss. Oh, Miss, Miss. I found this handkerchief there, and it belongs, I think, to my mother. She
has a heart condition and it might be serious for her to be
all alone. I don't think she has much money. And I'd like
to find her. Do you remember having seen her? She's on
her way to a town called Bountiful.

THELMA: Yes, I did see her. She was here talking to me. She
left all of a sudden.

LUDIE: Thank you so much.

(JESSIE MAE *comes into the terminal as* THELMA *starts out of the
terminal.*)

JESSIE MAE: Ludie.

LUDIE: I was right. She was here. The lady there saw her.

JESSIE MAE: Well, we are not going to wait.

LUDIE: That lady was talking to her.

JESSIE MAE: We're not going to wait. I've talked it all over
with the police.

LUDIE: You didn't really call them!

JESSIE MAE: I did. And they said in their opinion she was just
trying to get our attention this way and we should just go
home and pay her no mind at all. They say such things
are very common among young people and old people . . .

*EXTERIOR: STATION.*

MRS. WATTS *is at the window. She looks in at* LUDIE *and* JESSIE
MAE.

JESSIE MAE (*off camera*): . . . and they're positive that if we just
go home and show her that we don't care if she goes or
stays, she'll come home of her own free will.

*INTERIOR: BUS STATION.*

LUDIE *and* JESSIE MAE.

LUDIE: Jessie Mae . . .

JESSIE MAE: Now, we're going to do what the police tell us to
do. Now, Ludie, I wish you'd think of me for a change.
I'm not going to spend the rest of my life running after
your mother.

LUDIE: All right, Jessie Mae.

JESSIE MAE: Come on, let's go. Come on.

LUDIE: All right. But if Mama is not home in an hour I'm
going after her.

JESSIE MAE: All right.

(*They go out of the terminal.*)

*INTERIOR: ENTRANCE TO CAFE.*

MRS. WATTS *peers through the door watching to see if they have
gone.*

*INTERIOR: BUS STATION.*

MRS. WATTS *enters. She looks out the window and sees* JESSIE
MAE *and* LUDIE.

*EXTERIOR: BUS STOP.*

*A city bus is there.* JESSIE MAE *and* LUDIE *get on the bus and
ride off.*

*EXTERIOR: BUS STATION.*

THELMA *gets on a bus and finds a seat.* MRS. WATTS *gets on the
same bus and finds a seat by the window.*

*The bus going through the Houston streets.*

MRS. WATTS *watching from window of bus.*

*Bus going through Texas countryside.*

MRS. WATTS *watching from window of bus.*

*EXTERIOR: BUS STOP AT GAS STATION.*

*The bus pulls up.* THELMA *and* MRS. WATTS *and* BLACK WOMAN *among others get off with their luggage. The* BUS ATTENDANT *is there.*

BUS ATTENDANT (*to* THELMA): This one's yours? I'll get it.

THELMA: Thank you.

BLACK WOMAN: How long of a wait do we have?

BUS ATTENDANT: I'd say about an hour.

(*A pause. The* BLACK WOMAN *sighs.*)

   It can't be helped.

BLACK WOMAN: Oh, no Sir, no, I know it can't be helped. (*Sits on a bench.*) We have to take what comes.

(MRS. WATTS *and the others sit on the benches in front of the gas station. There is a full moon.* MRS. WATTS *looks over at the* BLACK WOMAN.)

MRS. WATTS: Do you have far to go?

BLACK WOMAN: Right far . . . Corpus.

BUS OPERATOR: You know what Corpus Christi means in Spanish?

MRS. WATTS: No, I don't.

BUS OPERATOR: Body of Christ.

MRS. WATTS: That so? I never heard that. (*To* BLACK WOMAN:) Did you?

BLACK WOMAN: No, I sure hasn't. The Body of Christ. Is that right?

(*A* MEXICAN MAN *waits at the other side of the bus stop.* BUS ATTENDANT *calls over to him.*)

BUS ATTENDANT: Is that right?

(*The* MEXICAN MAN *says something in Spanish.*)

BLACK WOMAN: I see the bus coming. I sure am glad to see it.

(*The bus pulls up and the people get on bus and then the bus moves off, leaving the* BUS ATTENDANT *alone. He goes into the station.*)

*INTERIOR: BUS.*

MRS. WATTS *and* THELMA *are seated next to each other.* MRS. WATTS *is by the window.*

MRS. WATTS: The bus is nice to ride, isn't it?

THELMA: It is.

MRS. WATTS: Excuse me for getting personal, but what's a pretty girl like you doing traveling alone?

THELMA: My husband has just been sent overseas. I'm going to stay with my family.

MRS. WATTS: I'm sorry to hear that. Well, you just say the Ninety-first Psalm over and over to yourself. It will be a bower of strength and protection for him. "He that dwelleth in the secret place of the most high shall abide under the shadow of the Almighty. I will say of my Lord, He is my refuge and my fortress . . ."

(THELMA *is crying.* MRS. WATTS *looks up and sees her.*)

I'm sorry, honey.

THELMA: I'm just lonesome for him, that's all.

MRS. WATTS: You keep him under the Lord's wing, and he'll be safe.

THELMA: Yes Ma'am. I'm sorry. I don't know what gets into me.

MRS. WATTS: Nobody needs to be ashamed of crying. We've all dampened our pillows sometime or other. I know I have.

THELMA: If I could only learn not to worry.

MRS. WATTS: I guess we all have wished that. Jessie Mae, my daughter-in-law, don't worry. "What for?" she says. Well, like I tell her, that's a fine attitude if you can cultivate it. Trouble is, I can't any longer.

THELMA: It is hard.

MRS. WATTS: I didn't used to worry. When I was a girl I was so carefree. Had lots to worry me, too. Everybody was so poor back in Bountiful. But we got along. I said to Papa once after our third crop failure in a row . . . whoever gave this place the name Bountiful? Said his papa did. Because in those days it was a land of plenty. You just had to drop seeds in the ground and the crops would spring up. We had cotton and corn and sugar cane. I still think it's the prettiest place I ever heard of. Jessie Mae says it's the ugliest. But she says that to bother me. She only saw it once, and then a rainy day at that. She says it's nothing but an old swamp. That may be, I said, but it's a mighty pretty swamp to me.

*EXTERIOR: BUS.*

*The bus goes through the Texas countryside.*

*INTERIOR: BUS.*

THELMA *is reading the movie magazine,* MRS. WATTS *her Bible.*
THELMA *puts her magazine down.*

THELMA: Mrs. Watts?

MRS. WATTS: Yes.

THELMA: I think I ought to tell you this. I . . . I don't want
you to think I'm interfering in your business, but well,
you see, your son and your daughter-in-law came in just
after you left . . .

MRS. WATTS: Oh, I know. I saw them coming. That's why I
left so fast.

THELMA: Your son seemed very concerned.

MRS. WATTS: Bless his heart.

THELMA: He found a handkerchief that you had dropped.

MRS. WATTS: That's right. I did.

THELMA: He asked me if I had seen you. I felt I had to say
yes. I wouldn't have said anything if he hadn't asked me.

MRS. WATTS: Oh, that's all right. I would have done the same
thing in your place. Did you talk to Jessie Mae?

THELMA: Yes.

MRS. WATTS: Isn't she a sight? I bet she told you I was crazy.

THELMA: Well . . .

MRS. WATTS: No. You needn't worry about it hurting my
feelings. Poor Jessie Mae, she thinks everybody's crazy
that don't want to sit in the beauty parlor all day and
drink Coca-Colas. You know, I think Ludie knows how I
feel about getting back to Bountiful, because once when
we were talkin' about something we did back there in the
old days, he burst out crying. He was so overcome he had
to leave the room.

*EXTERIOR: BUS.*

*The bus continues through the Texas countryside.*

*INTERIOR: BUS.*

THELMA *has her eyes closed.* MRS. WATTS *is looking out the window and humming.*

THELMA: That's a pretty hymn. What's the name of that?

MRS. WATTS: "There's Not a Friend Like the Lovely Jesus." Do you like hymns?

THELMA: Yes, I do.

MRS. WATTS: So do I. Jessie Mae says they've gone out of style, but I don't agree. What's your favorite hymn?

THELMA: I don't know.

MRS. WATTS: The one I was singing is mine. I bet I sing it a hundred times a day. When Jessie Mae isn't home. Hymns make Jessie Mae nervous. Jessie Mae hates me. I don't know why, but she hates me. Hate me or not, I gotta get back and smell that salt air and work that dirt. Callie said I could always come back and visit her and she meant it too. That's who I'm going to stay with now. Callie Davis. The whole first month of my visit I am going to work in Callie's garden. I haven't had my hands in dirt in twenty years. My hands feel the need of dirt. Do you like to work the land?

THELMA: I never have.

MRS. WATTS: Try it sometime. It'll do wonders for you. I bet I'll live to be a hundred. If I could just get outdoors. It was being cooped up in those two rooms that was killing me. I used to work the land like a man. Had to when Papa died. I got two little babies buried there. Renee Sue

and Douglas. Diphtheria got Renee Sue. I never knew
what carried Douglas away. He was just weak from the
start. I know that Callie's kept up their graves. Oh, if my
heart just holds out until I get there. Now, where do you
go after Harrison?

THELMA: Old Gulf. My family have just moved there from
Louisiana. I'll stay there with them until my husband
comes home again.

MRS. WATTS: That's nice.

THELMA: It'll be funny living at home again.

MRS. WATTS: How long have you been married?

THELMA: A year. My husband was anxious for me to go. He
said he'd worry about my being alone. I'm the only child
and my parents and I are very close.

MRS. WATTS: That's nice.

THELMA: I so hoped my mother and daddy would like my
husband and he'd like them. I needn't have worried.
They hit it off from the very first. Mother and Daddy say
they feel like they have two children now. A son and a
daughter.

MRS. WATTS: Isn't that nice. I've heard people say that when
your son marries you lose a son, but when your daughter
marries you get a son. What's your husband's name?

THELMA: Robert.

MRS. WATTS: That's a nice name.

THELMA: I think so. I guess any name he had I would think
was nice. I love my husband very much. Lots of girls I
know think I'm silly about him, but I can't help it.

MRS. WATTS: I wasn't in love with my husband. Do you
believe we are punished for the things we do wrong? I

sometimes think that's why I've had all my trouble. I've talked to many a preacher about it; all but one said they didn't think so. But I can't see any other reason. Of course, I didn't lie to my husband. I told him I didn't love him. That I admired him, which I did, but I didn't love him. That I'd never love anybody but Ray John Murray as long as I lived. And I didn't and I couldn't help it. Even when my husband died and I had to move back with Mama and Papa I used to sit on the front gallery every morning and every evening just to nod hello to Ray John Murray as he went by the house to work at the store. He went a mile out of his way to pass the house. He never loved nobody but me.

THELMA: Why didn't you marry him?

MRS. WATTS: Because his papa and my papa didn't speak. My papa forced me to write a letter saying I never wanted to see him again, and he got drunk and married out of spite. I felt sorry for his wife. She knew he never loved her. (*A pause.*) Well, I don't think about those things now. But they're all part of Bountiful. I think that's why I'm starting to think of them again. You're lucky to be married to the man you love.

THELMA: I know I am.

MRS. WATTS: Awfully lucky.

*EXTERIOR: BUS STATION—HARRISON. LATER THAT NIGHT.*

*The bus pulls up. The* DRIVER *is honking the horn.*

*INTERIOR: BUS STATION.*

*The* HARRISON TICKET MAN *is asleep at his desk. The bus horn wakes him.*

*EXTERIOR: BUS STATION.*

MRS. WATTS *and* THELMA *get off the bus.* THELMA *goes toward the station.* MRS. WATTS *stands outside on the porch.*

*INTERIOR: BUS STATION. NIGHT.*

HARRISON TICKET MAN *looks at his pocket watch as he leaves his office to meet the bus.*

*EXTERIOR: BUS STATION.*

MRS. WATTS *is on the porch.* THELMA *starts to go inside. The station lights come on.*

*INTERIOR: BUS STATION.*

HARRISON TICKET MAN *turns around and sees* THELMA *struggling with the door. She sets down a suitcase and opens the door, picks up the suitcase and enters the station.*

HARRISON TICKET MAN: Want any help with those bags?

THELMA: No, thank you.

(HARRISON TICKET MAN *gets a luggage dolly and starts toward door.*)

    Excuse me?

HARRISON TICKET MAN: Yes?

THELMA: Is the bus to Old Gulf going to be on time?

HARRISON TICKET MAN: Always is.

*EXTERIOR: BUS STATION.*

HARRISON TICKET MAN *pushes the luggage dolly outside. The bus drives off.* MRS. WATTS *goes inside the station. The* HARRISON TICKET MAN *loads packages onto the dolly.* MRS. WATTS *and* THELMA *can be seen through the station windows.*

MRS. WATTS: What time is it, honey?

THELMA: Ten o'clock.

MRS. WATTS: Ten o'clock. I bet Callie will be surprised to see me walk in at ten o'clock.

THELMA: Did you tell her you were coming today?

*INTERIOR: BUS STATION.*

MRS. WATTS *and* THELMA *are sitting on a bench.*

MRS. WATTS: No. I couldn't. Because I didn't know. I had to wait until Jessie Mae went out to the drugstore.

THELMA: My bus leaves in half an hour.

MRS. WATTS: Oh, I see. I'd better be finding out how I'm going to get on out to Bountiful.

(MRS. WATTS *gets up.* THELMA *gets up and stops her.*)

THELMA: No, you sit down, sit down. I'll find the man.

(THELMA *goes outside.* MRS. WATTS *follows her to the door and listens.*)

*EXTERIOR: BUS STATION.*

HARRISON TICKET MAN *is still loading packages onto the dolly as* THELMA *comes out to him.*

THELMA: Excuse me again.

HARRISON TICKET MAN: Yes?

THELMA: My friend here wants to know how she can get to Bountiful.

HARRISON TICKET MAN: Bountiful?

THELMA: Yes.

(MRS. WATTS *comes outside.*)

HARRISON TICKET MAN: What's she going there for?

(MRS. WATTS *comes up to the* HARRISON TICKET MAN.)

MRS. WATTS: I'm going to visit my girlhood friend.

HARRISON TICKET MAN: I don't know who that's gonna be. The last person in Bountiful was Mrs. Callie Davis. She died day before yesterday. That is, they found her day before yesterday. She lived all alone so they don't know exactly when she died. Excuse me. (*Lifts dolly and pushes it toward the door.*)

MRS. WATTS: Callie Davis!

HARRISON TICKET MAN: Yes Ma'am. They had the funeral this morning. Was she the one you were going to visit?

MRS. WATTS: Yessir. That's the one. She was my friend. My girlhood friend.

(HARRISON TICKET MAN *goes inside the station.* MRS. WATTS *stands for a moment. Then she sits on the bench.* THELMA *goes inside to the* HARRISON TICKET MAN.)

THELMA: Is there a hotel here?

HARRISON TICKET MAN: Oh, yes'm. The Riverview.

THELMA: How far is it?

HARRISON TICKET MAN: About three blocks.

THELMA (*coming outside to* MRS. WATTS): What'll you do now, Mrs. Watts?

MRS. WATTS: I'm thinking, honey. I'm thinking.

(*She pauses.* THELMA *sits down on bench beside her.*)

It's come to me what to do. I'll go on. That much has come to me. I'll go on. I feel my strength and my purpose strong within me. I'll go on to Bountiful. I will walk those twelve miles if I have to.

THELMA: Now, Mrs. Watts, what are you going to do if there's no one out there? What'll you do this time of night?

MRS. WATTS: Oh, yes. I guess you're right.

THELMA: I think you should wait until morning.

MRS. WATTS: Yes. I guess I should. And then I can hire somebody to drive me out. You know what I'll do? (*Gets up and walks around.*) I'll stay at my own house, or what's left of it. You put me in a garden and I'll get along fine with the help of my government checks.

(MRS. WATTS *starts to go inside.* THELMA *gets up and stops her.*)

THELMA: Mrs. Watts, the man says there's a hotel not too far from here. I think you'd better let me take you there.

MRS. WATTS: Oh, no thank you. I'm not going to waste my money on a hotel. They're as high as cats' backs, you know. I'll just sleep right there on the bench.

*INTERIOR: BUS STATION.*

THELMA *and* MRS. WATTS *come inside.* MRS. WATTS *goes toward a bench.*

MRS. WATTS: I'll put my coat under my head, hold my purse under my arm . . . (*Begins to look around for her purse.*) My purse! Honey, did you see my purse? (*Begins to search frantically for the purse.*)

THELMA: Why, no . . .

(THELMA *and* MRS. WATTS *go back to the ticket window. The* HARRISON TICKET MAN *is asleep at his desk.*)

Excuse me.

HARRISON TICKET MAN: Yeah.

THELMA: This lady left her purse on the bus.

HARRISON TICKET MAN: All right. I'll call ahead about it. How can you identify it?

MRS. WATTS: It's a plain brown purse.

HARRISON TICKET MAN: How much money?

MRS. WATTS: Thirty-five cents and a pension check.

HARRISON TICKET MAN: Who was the check made out to?

MRS. WATTS: To me.

THELMA: Mrs. . . .

MRS. WATTS: Mrs. Carrie Watts.

HARRISON TICKET MAN: All right. I'll call up about it.

MRS. WATTS: Thank you. That's most kind.

THELMA: How long will it take to get it back?

HARRISON TICKET MAN: Well, depends. If I can get ahead of the bus at Don Tarle . . . they can send it back on the Victoria bus and it should be here in a couple of hours.

MRS. WATTS: That's awful kind of you.

(*He goes to the phone. They go back to the bench.*)

THELMA: Try not to worry about the purse.

MRS. WATTS: I won't. I'm too tired to worry. Be time enough to start worrying when I wake up in the morning.

(MRS. WATTS *sits down on bench.* THELMA *folds Mrs. Watts' coat and puts it on the bench.*)

THELMA: Why don't you see if you can go on to sleep now.

MRS. WATTS: Oh, no. I thought I'd stay up and see you off.

THELMA: Oh, no. You go on to sleep.

MRS. WATTS: I couldn't go right off to sleep now. I'm too wound up. You know I don't go on a trip every day of my life.

HARRISON TICKET MAN (*calling out to them*): You're lucky. Bus hadn't gotten to Don Tarle yet. If they can find the purse it'll be here around twelve.

THELMA: Make you feel better?

MRS. WATTS: Yes, it does. Of course, everything has seemed to work out today. Why is it some days everything works out, and other days nothing works out? What I mean is, I've been trying to get to Bountiful for over five years. Now usually Jessie Mae and Ludie come find me before I ever get inside the railroad station good. Today, I got inside, both the railroad station and the bus station. I bought a ticket. I seen Ludie and Jessie Mae before they saw me. I hid out. Met a pretty friend like you. I lost my purse, and now I have somebody finding it for me. I guess the Lord is with me today. I wonder why the Lord is not with us every day? Sure would be so nice if He was. Maybe then we wouldn't appreciate so much the days when He is with us. Or maybe He's with us always, and we don't know it. Maybe I had to wait twenty years cooped up in a city before I could appreciate getting back here. (*Starts to sing a hymn.*)

> Blessed assurance, Jesus is mine.
> Oh, what a foretaste of glory divine.
> Heir of salvation, purchase of God
> Born of His Spirit, washed in His blood.

(*She pauses.*) Oh, isn't it nice to be able to sing a hymn when you want to. (*Begins singing again.*)

This is my story, this is my song,
Praising my Saviour, all the day long . . .

(THELMA *joins her in singing.*)

MRS. WATTS *and* THELMA (*singing*):
This is my story, this is my song.
Praising my Saviour all the day long.

(*A pause.*)

MRS. WATTS: I'm a happy woman, young lady. I'm a very happy woman.

THELMA: I still have a sandwich left.

(MRS. WATTS *watches her pull a sandwich from her bag.*)
Will you have one?

MRS. WATTS: Sure you don't want it?

THELMA: No, I'm full.

MRS. WATTS (*taking the sandwich*): I'll just take a half.

THELMA: Take the whole thing. I'm not hungry.

MRS. WATTS: No, no. Just the half. Thank you. You know I don't eat much. Particularly if I'm excited.

(*She rises and stands nibbling on the sandwich. She goes out onto the porch.* THELMA *follows.*)

*EXTERIOR: BUS STATION.*

MRS. WATTS *and* THELMA *come outside.*

MRS. WATTS: You know, I came to my first dance in this town.

THELMA: Did you?

MRS. WATTS: Yes Ma'am. It was the summertime. And my father couldn't decide if he thought dancing was right or not. But my mother said she had danced when she was a girl, and I was gonna dance. And so I went. The girls from all over the county came for this dance. It was at the Opera House. I can't remember what the occasion was, but it was something special. Do you know something, young lady? If my daughter had lived, I would have wanted her to be just like you.

THELMA: Oh, thank you.

MRS. WATTS: Sweet and considerate and thoughtful. And pretty.

THELMA: Thank you.

HARRISON TICKET MAN (*coming out to the porch*): You'd better get your suitcase, Miss. Bus will be up the road. He won't wait this time of night.

THELMA: All right.

(THELMA *goes inside. The* HARRISON TICKET MAN *checks his watch.*)

MRS. WATTS: I was just telling my little friend here that I came to my first dance in this town.

HARRISON TICKET MAN: That right?

MRS. WATTS: Yes. I've been to Harrison quite a few times in my life shopping.

(*The bus rounds the corner.* MRS. WATTS *waves it down.* THELMA *runs back with her suitcase.*)

THELMA: Goodbye, Mrs. Watts.

MRS. WATTS: Goodbye, honey. Good luck to you.

THELMA: Good luck to you.

(THELMA *gets onto the bus.* MRS. WATTS *waves as it goes, then she comes up onto the porch with the* HARRISON TICKET MAN.)

HARRISON TICKET MAN: Are you gonna stay here all night?

MRS. WATTS: I have to. Everything I have is on the bus. We can't go any place without money.

HARRISON TICKET MAN: I guess that's right.

(MRS. WATTS *follows the* HARRISON TICKET MAN *inside the station.*)

*INTERIOR: BUS STATION.*

MRS. WATTS *and the* HARRISON TICKET MAN *are there.*

MRS. WATTS: Do they still have dances in Borden's Opera House?

HARRISON TICKET MAN: No Ma'am. It's torn down. They condemned it, you know. Did you know anybody in Harrison?

MRS. WATTS: I knew a few people when I was a girl. (*Sits down on the bench.*) Priscilla Nytelle. Did you know her?

HARRISON TICKET MAN (*begins turning off the lights*): No Ma'am.

MRS. WATTS: Nancy Lee Goodhue?

HARRISON TICKET MAN: No Ma'am.

MRS. WATTS: The Fay girls?

HARRISON TICKET MAN: No Ma'am.

MRS. WATTS: I used to trade in Mr. Ewing's store. I knew him to speak to.

HARRISON TICKET MAN: Which Ewing was that?

MRS. WATTS: George White Ewing.

HARRISON TICKET MAN: He's dead.

MRS. WATTS: That so?

HARRISON TICKET MAN: Been dead for twelve years.

MRS. WATTS: That so?

HARRISON TICKET MAN: He left quite a bit of money, but his son took over his store and lost it all. Drank.

MRS. WATTS: Is that so? One thing I can say about my boy is that he never gave me any trouble that way.

HARRISON TICKET MAN: Well, that's good. I've got one boy that drinks and one boy that doesn't. I can't understand it, raised them the same way.

MRS. WATTS: I know. I've known of other cases like that. One drinks. The other doesn't.

HARRISON TICKET MAN (*going into his office*): A friend of mine has a girl that drinks. I think that's the saddest thing in the world.

MRS. WATTS: Isn't it?

HARRISON TICKET MAN: Well. Good night.

MRS. WATTS: Good night.

*EXTERIOR: BUS STATION. NIGHT.*

*The street is deserted. Lights inside the station go off.*

*INTERIOR: BUS STATION.*

MRS. WATTS *is lying on the bench holding her Bible and softly humming a hymn.*

*INTERIOR: SHERIFF'S CAR.*

*The* SHERIFF *drives up to the bus station and gets out of his car.*

*INTERIOR: BUS STATION.*

*The* SHERIFF *comes into the bus station. He sees* MRS. WATTS *lying on the bench asleep. The* SHERIFF *goes to the* HARRISON TICKET MAN, *who is asleep at his desk.*

SHERIFF: Roy? Come on, Roy, wake up.

HARRISON TICKET MAN (*opening his eyes*): Oh, hello, Sheriff.

SHERIFF: How long has this old woman been here?

HARRISON TICKET MAN (*looking at his watch*): About six hours.

SHERIFF: Did she get off the bus from Houston?

HARRISON TICKET MAN: Yessir. I know her name. It's Watts. She left her purse on the bus and I had to call up to Don Tarle about it.

SHERIFF: You have her purse.

HARRISON TICKET MAN: Yes. It just came.

(*The* HARRISON TICKET MAN *gets the purse and gives it to the* SHERIFF. *The* SHERIFF *looks inside.*)

SHERIFF: She's the one, all right. I've had a call from the Houston police to hold her until her son can come for her.

HARRISON TICKET MAN: She said she used to live in Bountiful.

(*The* SHERIFF *starts over to her to wake her up. He comes back to the* HARRISON TICKET MAN *and returns the purse to him.*)

SHERIFF: Poor thing. Sleeping so sound. I don't have the heart to wake her up. Tell you what, I'll go over to my office, call Houston, tell them she's here. Her son is coming in his car. He should be here around seven-thirty. I'll be back in ten minutes. Now Roy, if she gives you any trouble, you just call me. You keep your eye on her.

HARRISON TICKET MAN: All right.

(*The* SHERIFF *goes out and the screen door bangs. This wakes* MRS. WATTS. *She opens her eyes and looks around trying to remember where she is.*)

MRS. WATTS: Good morning.

HARRISON TICKET MAN: Good morning.

MRS. WATTS: Did my purse arrive?

HARRISON TICKET MAN: Yes Ma'am.

MRS. WATTS: Oh, thank you so much.

(*He hands the purse to her.*)

I wonder if you could cash a check for me?

HARRISON TICKET MAN: I'm sorry, Ma'am. I can't.

MRS. WATTS: It's a government check and I have identification.

HARRISON TICKET MAN: I'm sorry, Ma'am. I can't.

MRS. WATTS: Well, do you know where I could get a check cashed?

HARRISON TICKET MAN: Why?

MRS. WATTS: Why? I need money to get me started in Bountiful. I want to hire someone to drive me out there and look at my house and get a few groceries. Try to find a cot to sleep on.

HARRISON TICKET MAN: I'm sorry, lady, you're not going to Bountiful.

MRS. WATTS: Oh, yes I am.

HARRISON TICKET MAN: I have to hold you here for the sheriff.

MRS. WATTS: You are joking with me? Don't joke with me. I have come too far.

HARRISON TICKET MAN: I need to keep you here until your son arrives in his car this morning.

MRS. WATTS: My son hasn't got a car, so I don't believe you.

HARRISON TICKET MAN: The sheriff will be here in a minute and you can ask him yourself.

MRS. WATTS: All right. But I'm going.

(HARRISON TICKET MAN *watches her as she goes back to the bench.*)

> Do you understand that? You'll see. This is a free country. And I'll tell him that. And no sheriff, or king, or president is going to keep me from going back to Bountiful.

HARRISON TICKET MAN: All right. You tell him that.

(MRS. WATTS *sits down. The* HARRISON TICKET MAN *walks away from the door.*)

MRS. WATTS: What time is my son expected?

HARRISON TICKET MAN: Around seven-thirty.

(HARRISON TICKET MAN *straightens up the waiting area.* MRS. WATTS *picks up her suitcase and starts toward the door.*)

MRS. WATTS: Where can I find me a driver?

(HARRISON TICKET MAN *watches her carefully and positions himself between her and the door.*)

> I can make it to Bountiful and back way before seven-thirty.

HARRISON TICKET MAN: Look, lady . . .

MRS. WATTS: That's all I want. Just to see it. Just to stand on the porch of my own house again.

HARRISON TICKET MAN: Lady, I don't have any . . .

MRS. WATTS: I thought last night, I had to stay, I thought

I'd die if I couldn't stay. But now, I'll settle for less. An hour. A half hour. Fifteen minutes.

HARRISON TICKET MAN: Lady, it ain't up to me. I told you the sheriff . . .

MRS. WATTS: Then get me the sheriff!

HARRISON TICKET MAN: Look, lady . . .

MRS. WATTS: Get me the sheriff. The time is going. They're going to have me locked in those two rooms again soon. The time is going. The time is going . . .

(*The* SHERIFF *comes in. He goes over to* MRS. WATTS.)

SHERIFF: Mrs. Watts?

MRS. WATTS: Yessir. Are you the sheriff?

SHERIFF: Yes Ma'am.

MRS. WATTS: I understand that my son will be here at seven-thirty to take me back to Houston.

SHERIFF: Yes Ma'am.

MRS. WATTS: Then listen to me, Sir. I have made myself one promise. To see my home again before I die.

SHERIFF: Lady, I . . .

MRS. WATTS: Now, I'm not asking that I not go back. I'm willing to go back. Just let me go these twelve miles now. I have money. I can pay.

SHERIFF: That's between you and your son, Ma'am.

MRS. WATTS: Ludie? Why, he's got to do whatever Jessie Mae tells him to do. I know why she wants me back. It's for my government check. (*Gets her suitcase and goes back to bench.*)

SHERIFF: I don't know anything about that, Ma'am.

MRS. WATTS: Won't you let me go?

SHERIFF: Not unless your son takes you.

MRS. WATTS: All right, then. I've lost. (*Drops her suitcase.*) I've come all this way only to lose. (*Drops her purse and coat on bench.*) I'm going to die and Jessie Mae knows that. And she's willful and it's her will I die in those two rooms. Well, she's not going to have her way. It is my will to die in Bountiful.

(*She starts to run out of the bus station. The* SHERIFF *stops her.*)

Let me go those twelve miles . . . before it's too late. Understand me. Suffering I don't mind. Suffering I understand. I didn't protest once! Even though my heart was broken when those babies died. But these fifteen years of bickering, of endless, petty bickering. It's made me like Jessie Mae sees me. It's ugly. I will not be that way. I want to go home. I want to go home.

(SHERIFF *takes hold of her as she almost collapses. He helps her over to the bench and settles her there.*)

SHERIFF (*to the* HARRISON TICKET MAN): Hey, Roy.

HARRISON TICKET MAN: Yes Sir.

SHERIFF: Get a doctor.

MRS. WATTS: I'm all right.

SHERIFF: Hurry.

HARRISON TICKET MAN: Yes Sir.

MRS. WATTS: No doctor. Bountiful . . .

(SHERIFF *helps* MRS. WATTS *lie down.*)

SHERIFF: Just lie down. Just lie down. It's all right.

*INTERIOR: BUS STATION.*

MRS. WATTS *is sitting on the bench.* DR. WHITE *is on the porch talking to the* SHERIFF. *The* DOCTOR *leaves, and the* SHERIFF *comes back in.*

SHERIFF: Mrs. Watts.

MRS. WATTS: Yessir . . .

SHERIFF: How are you feeling?

MRS. WATTS: Stronger by the minute, thank you.

SHERIFF: The doctor said we are to keep you calm, and see that you rest until your son gets here.

MRS. WATTS: Thank you. I appreciate your interest.

SHERIFF: But he said he didn't think it would do any harm if I wanted to drive you out to your place, as long as you felt well enough to go.

MRS. WATTS: Yessir . . . thank you. I feel well enough to go.

SHERIFF: All right, I'll take you.

*EXTERIOR: COUNTRYSIDE. DAY.*

*The* SHERIFF *and* MRS. WATTS *are in his car driving over a country road.*

*INTERIOR: CAR.*

SHERIFF *is driving.* MRS. WATTS *gazes out the windows at the land as they ride.*

*EXTERIOR: COUNTRYSIDE.*

*The car with the* SHERIFF *and* MRS. WATTS *continues on.*

*INTERIOR: CAR.*

MRS. WATTS *and the* SHERIFF.

MRS. WATTS: Oh . . .

SHERIFF: This look familiar?

MRS. WATTS: Surely does.

*EXTERIOR: STREET IN HARRISON. DAY.*

LUDIE *and* JESSIE MAE *drive up to the bus station. They get out of the car and start toward station.*

*EXTERIOR: COUNTRYSIDE.*

*Sheriff's car continues driving along the road.*

*INTERIOR: SHERIFF'S CAR.*

MRS. WATTS *looks out at what is left of the town of Bountiful.*

*EXTERIOR: BOUNTIFUL.*

*Deserted houses and stores are passed as the car goes through the town.*

*INTERIOR: SHERIFF'S CAR.*

MRS. WATTS *and the* SHERIFF.

MRS. WATTS: My lord . . . look at Bountiful, there's nothing left.

*EXTERIOR: BOUNTIFUL.*

*The car continues past the deserted houses and stores.*

*INTERIOR: SHERIFF'S CAR.*

MRS. WATTS *looking out.*

*EXTERIOR: COUNTRYSIDE.*

*They continue driving through countryside.*

*INTERIOR: SHERIFF'S CAR.*

SHERIFF *is driving.* MRS. WATTS *looks around at the countryside.*

*EXTERIOR: SHERIFF'S CAR.*

*They turn off road and drive up the lane leading to her house. They can only drive part of the way in as the road is grown up with brush and scrub trees.*

*INTERIOR: SHERIFF'S CAR.*

MRS. WATTS *is busy looking around.*

*EXTERIOR: SHERIFF'S CAR.*

*The* SHERIFF *parks the car and gets out and opens the car door for her. She gets out and slowly they walk up the lane toward her house. It is a two-story house badly in need of paint and repair. It is surrounded by trees and brush.*

MRS. WATTS: I'm home. I'm home. Thank you.

*(They continue slowly toward the house until they reach the back porch.)*

SHERIFF: You'd better come over here. Sit down for a while.

(MRS. WATTS *sits down on the porch.*)

> You don't want to overdo it. Are you feeling all right now?

MRS. WATTS: Yes I am. I feel ever so much better.

SHERIFF: Why, you look better. I hope I've done the right thing in bringing you here. (*Sits down on the edge of the porch.*)

MRS. WATTS: Thank you. You have been very kind.

(*A bird calls.*)

> What kind of bird is that?

SHERIFF: That's an old redbird.

MRS. WATTS: I thought that was a redbird, but it's been so long since I heard one I couldn't be sure. Do they still have scissortails around here?

SHERIFF: Yes Ma'am. I still see one every once in a while, when I'm driving around the country.

MRS. WATTS: I don't know anything prettier than a scissortail flying around in the sky. You know, my father was a good man, in many ways. A peculiar man, but a good one. And one thing he couldn't stand was to see a bird shot on his land. If he saw men coming here hunting, he'd just take his gun and chase them away. And I think the birds knew they couldn't be touched here. Ours was always home to them. We had ducks and geese . . . finches, blue jays, bluebirds, and redbirds.

SHERIFF: Ricebirds. They're getting thicker every year. They seem to thrive out here on the coast.

MRS. WATTS: I think a mockingbird is my favorite of them all.

SHERIFF: I think it's mine, too.

MRS. WATTS: I don't know, though. I'm mighty partial to the scissortail. I hope I see one soon.

SHERIFF: I hope you can.

MRS. WATTS: You know, my father was born on this land and in this house. Did you know my father?

SHERIFF: No Ma'am. Not that I can remember.

MRS. WATTS: I guess there are not many around here who remember my father. I do. Of course, and my son. Maybe some old-timers around Harrison. You know it's funny but ever since we've got here I just . . . I have half the feeling that my father and my mother would come out of this house, greet me, and welcome me home. Well, I guess when you've lived longer than your house or your family, you've lived long enough. (*Gets up and looks around.*) But what happened to the farms? For the last five miles I've seen nothing but empty fields.

SHERIFF: I know. The land around Bountiful just played out. People like you got discouraged and moved away.

MRS. WATTS: Callie Davis kept her farm going.

SHERIFF: Yes, she did. She learned how to treat her land right and it began paying off for her toward the end. I've heard she was out riding her tractor the day before she died. Yes, a lonely death she had. All by herself in that big house.

MRS. WATTS: There are worse things.

SHERIFF: Looks to me like you're going to have a pretty day.

MRS. WATTS: I hope so.

SHERIFF: You feeling more rested now?

MRS. WATTS: Oh, yes, I am.

SHERIFF: Well, I'm gonna go on back to my car. Now, you call me if you need anything. Anything.

MRS. WATTS: Thank you.

(*The* SHERIFF *turns and walks through the yard back toward his car.* MRS. WATTS *watches him and then gets up and looks around the porch. She touches the wooden boards of the house.*)

*INTERIOR: WATTS HOUSE.*

MRS. WATTS *comes into the house and pauses to look around. There is not much in the house downstairs except for a rusted child's tractor in a corner of one of the rooms.* MRS. WATTS *slowly goes from room to room. She pauses at the fireplace in what once was the parlor and puts her purse on the mantle. She then goes toward the stairs leading to the upstairs bedroom.*

*INTERIOR: UPSTAIRS BEDROOM.*

MRS. WATTS *enters room and sees an old bed frame; she looks out the window.*

LUDIE (*off camera*): Mama.

*EXTERIOR: WATTS HOUSE.*

LUDIE *is walking toward the house, calling.* MRS. WATTS *is at the window and turns away.* LUDIE *continues coming toward the house.*

LUDIE (*calling*): Mama? Mama?

*EXTERIOR: FRONT PORCH OF THE HOUSE.*

MRS. WATTS *is there sitting in a chair.* LUDIE *comes around the corner of the porch from the backyard.*

LUDIE: Hello, Mama.

MRS. WATTS: Hello, Son.

LUDIE: How do you feel?

MRS. WATTS: I feel much better, Ludie.

LUDIE: Yes'm.

MRS. WATTS: I got my wish.

LUDIE: Yes Ma'am.

MRS. WATTS: I hope I didn't worry you too much, Ludie. But I just felt I had . . .

LUDIE: I know, Mama.

MRS. WATTS: You see, Son, I know it's hard for you to understand and Jessie Mae to understand.

LUDIE: Yes Ma'am. I understand, Mama. It's done now. So let's just forget about it.

MRS. WATTS: All right, Sonny. You did bring Jessie Mae, didn't you?

LUDIE: Yes Ma'am.

MRS. WATTS: Well, now she's here, isn't she going to get out of the car and look around a little?

LUDIE: Oh, well, she didn't seem to want to, Mama.

MRS. WATTS: You asked her?

LUDIE: Yes Ma'am.

MRS. WATTS: Did you ask about your raise, Son?

LUDIE: Yes Ma'am. Mr. Douglas said he liked my work and he'd be glad to recommend a raise for me.

MRS. WATTS: The sky's so blue, Ludie. Did you ever see the sky so blue?

LUDIE: No Ma'am.

MRS. WATTS: You know, Callie Davis died?

LUDIE: Is that so? When did that happen?

MRS. WATTS: Well, they don't rightly know. They found her dead. She'd been riding a tractor the day before they found her. They buried her yesterday.

LUDIE: Mama, I should have made myself bring you out here sooner. I'm sorry. I just thought it would be easier if we never see the house again.

MRS. WATTS: I know, Ludie. But, now that you're here, wouldn't you like to come inside, Son, and look around? (*Gets up and starts to go inside the house.*)

LUDIE: I don't think I better, Mama. I don't see any use in it. I'd rather remember it like it was.

MRS. WATTS: The old house has gotten kind of run down, hasn't it? I don't think it's gonna last out the next Gulf storm.

LUDIE: It doesn't look like it would.

MRS. WATTS: You know who you look like standing there?

LUDIE: Who?

MRS. WATTS: My papa.

LUDIE: I do?

MRS. WATTS: Just like him. Of course, I've been noticing as you been getting older that you look more and more like him. My papa was a good-looking man.

LUDIE: He was?

MRS. WATTS: Well, you've seen his pictures. Didn't you think so?

LUDIE: I don't remember. It's been so long since I looked at his pictures.

MRS. WATTS: He was always considered a very nice-looking man. Do you remember my papa at all, Sonny?

LUDIE: No Ma'am. Not too well. I was only ten when he died, Mama. I remember the day he died. I heard about it as I was coming home from school. Lee Weems told me. I thought he was joking and I called him a liar. I remember you took me into the parlor there, the day of the funeral, to say goodbye to him. I remember the coffin and the people sitting in the room. Old man, Joe Weems . . . Joe Weems took me up to his knee and told me that Grandpa was his best friend and that his life was a real example for me to follow. I remember Grandma sitting by the coffin crying, and she made me promise that when I had a son of my own I'd name it after Grandpa. I would too. I've never forgotten that promise. Well, I didn't have a son or a daughter.

(MRS. WATTS *sits down on the edge of the porch.*)

Billy Davis told me today that his wife is expecting her fourth child. They already have two girls and a son. Billy Davis doesn't make much more than I do, and they certainly seem to get along. They have their own house and a car. Why, it does your heart good to hear them tell about how they all get along. Everybody has their own job, even the youngest child. She's only three. She puts the napkins around the table at mealtimes. That's her job! Billy said to me, Ludie, I don't know if I could get along without my kids. He said, I don't know how you get along, Ludie. What you work for. I said, well, Billy . . . (*Pause.*) I haven't made any kind of life for you, Mama, either of you, and I try so hard. Mama, I lied to you. I do remember, I remember so much. This house with the life here. The night you woke me up and dressed me and took me for a walk when the moon was full, and I cried because I was scared and you comforted me. Mama, I want to stop remembering. It doesn't do any good remembering.

(*The car horn is heard.*)

That's Jessie Mae.

*EXTERIOR: CAR.*

JESSIE MAE *is in the car.*

*EXTERIOR: HOUSE.*

LUDIE (*going to his mother*): We have to start back now, Mama.

(LUDIE *and* MRS. WATTS *start to walk toward the car.* MRS. WATTS *turns to sit back down. She begins to cry.* LUDIE *sits down beside her.*)

MRS. WATTS: Oh, Ludie, what has happened to us? Why have we come to this?

LUDIE: I don't know, Mama.

MRS. WATTS: To have stayed and fought the land would have been better than this.

LUDIE: Yes'm.

MRS. WATTS: Pretty soon, all this will be gone. Twenty years, ten, this house, me, you . . .

LUDIE: I know, Mama.

MRS. WATTS: But the river will still be here. The fields, the trees, and the smell of the Gulf. I always got my strength from that. Not from houses, not from people. It's so quiet. So eternally quiet. I'd forgotten the peace and the quiet. (*Points out into the distance.*) Do you remember how my papa always had that field over there planted in cotton?

LUDIE: Yes, Mama.

MRS. WATTS: You see, it's all woods now. But I expect some-day people will come and cut down the trees and plant the cotton, and maybe even wear out the land again, and then their children will sell it and move to the cities, and trees will come up again.

LUDIE: I expect so, Mama.

MRS. WATTS: We're part of all that. We left it, but we can never lose what it's given us.

LUDIE: I expect so, Mama.

JESSIE MAE (*calling from the field*): Ludie. Are you coming or not?

LUDIE: We were just startin', Jessie Mae.

MRS. WATTS: Hello . . . Jessie Mae.

JESSIE MAE (*continues making her way to the house*): I'm not speaking to you. I guess you're proud of the time you gave us, dragging us here, this time of the morning. If Ludie loses his job over this, I hope you're satisfied.

LUDIE: I'm not going to lose my job, Jessie Mae.

JESSIE MAE: Well, you could.

LUDIE: All right, Jessie Mae.

JESSIE MAE: And she should realize that. She's selfish. That's her trouble. Always has been. Just pure deep selfish. Did you tell your mama what we were discussing in the car?

LUDIE: No. We can talk it all over driving back to Houston.

JESSIE MAE: I think we should have it all out right here. I would like everything understood right now. I have it written down. Do you want to read it or do you want me to read it to you, Mother Watts?

MRS. WATTS: What is it, Jessie Mae?

JESSIE MAE: It's a few rules and regulations that are necessary to my peace of mind. And I think to Ludie's. First of all, I'd like to ask you a question.

MRS. WATTS: Yes Ma'am.

JESSIE MAE: Didn't you know you'd be caught and have to come back?

MRS. WATTS: I had to come, Jessie Mae. Twenty years is a long time.

JESSIE MAE: Didn't you know you could have died?

MRS. WATTS: I knew.

JESSIE MAE: And you didn't care?

MRS. WATTS: I had to come, Jessie Mae.

JESSIE MAE: I hope it's out of your system now.

MRS. WATTS: It is. I've had my trip. That's more than enough to keep me happy for the rest of my life.

JESSIE MAE: Well, I'm glad to hear it. That's the first thing on my list. (*Reads from the list.*) There will be no more running away.

MRS. WATTS: There will be no more running away.

JESSIE MAE: Good. Number two, no more hymn singing . . .

(MRS. WATTS *turns and looks at* JESSIE MAE.)

. . . when I'm in the apartment. When I'm gone you can sing your lungs out. Agreed?

MRS. WATTS: Agreed.

JESSIE MAE: Number three.

LUDIE: Jessie Mae, can't this wait till we get home?

JESSIE MAE: Now, honey, we agreed that I'm going to handle this! No more pouting. When I ask a question, I'd like an answer. Otherwise, I'll consider it pouting.

MRS. WATTS: All right.

JESSIE MAE: Number four. With your heart in the condition that it's in, I feel you should not run around the apartment when you can walk.

MRS. WATTS: All right, Jessie Mae.

JESSIE MAE: Is there anything you want to say to me?

MRS. WATTS: No, Jessie Mae.

JESSIE MAE: I might as well tell you right now, I'm not staying in the house and watching over you anymore, I am joining a bridge club and I'm going to town at least twice a week. (*Puts the list away.*)

LUDIE: We also agreed to try to get along. Jessie Mae also realizes that sometimes she gets upset when she shouldn't. Don't you, Jessie Mae?

JESSIE MAE: Uh huh.

LUDIE: So, let's start by trying to have a pleasant ride home.

JESSIE MAE: All rightie. Is there any water around here? I'm thirsty.

LUDIE: I don't think so, Jessie Mae. Is there any water around here, Mama?

MRS. WATTS: The cistern is gone.

JESSIE MAE: Look at my shoes! They have scratches on them. They're my good pair. I ought to have my head examined for wearing my only good pair of shoes out here in this old swamp.

LUDIE: When I was a boy, Jessie Mae, I used to drink in the creek over there.

JESSIE MAE: Well, you wouldn't catch me drinking out of any creek. I knew a man once that went on a hunting trip, and drank out of a creek and caught something and died.

MRS. WATTS: There's nothing like cistern water for washing your hair with.

JESSIE MAE: Come on. Let's get going. Do we go back by way of Harrison?

LUDIE: Uh huh.

JESSIE MAE: Good. Then we can stop at the drugstore. I'm so thirsty I could drink ten Coca-Colas. Are you ready?

MRS. WATTS: Yes'm.

JESSIE MAE: Where's your purse?

MRS. WATTS: Are you talking to me, Jessie Mae?

JESSIE MAE: Who else would I be talking to? Since when did Ludie start going around with a pocketbook under his arm?

MRS. WATTS (*looking around*): I guess I left it inside.

JESSIE MAE: Where?

MRS. WATTS: I'll go get it.

JESSIE MAE: No. I want to go. You'll take all day. You wait here.

(*She goes inside the house.* LUDIE *and* MRS. WATTS *start walking back toward the car.*)

LUDIE: Mama . . .

MRS. WATTS: It's all right, Ludie, Son.

JESSIE MAE (*coming out with purse*): Here! Here's your purse. Now, where is that money for that government check?

MRS. WATTS: I didn't cash it. It's right inside the purse.

JESSIE MAE (*opening the purse and beginning to search through it*): No. It isn't.

MRS. WATTS: Let me look. (*Rummages around. She begins to laugh.*)

JESSIE MAE: What's the matter with you?

MRS. WATTS: That's a good joke on me.

JESSIE MAE: Well, what's so funny?

MRS. WATTS: I just remembered. I left this purse on the bus last night, and I caused a man a lot of trouble because I thought the check was in it. And do you know that check wasn't in that purse all that time?

JESSIE MAE: Where was it?

MRS. WATTS: It was in here. It's been in here since yesterday afternoon.

(*She reaches inside her dress and takes it out.* JESSIE MAE *reaches for the check.*)

JESSIE MAE: Well, give it to me before you go and lose it again.

MRS. WATTS: I'm not gonna lose it.

JESSIE MAE: Now don't start that business again. Just give it to me.

LUDIE: Jessie Mae.

JESSIE MAE (*grabbing the check from* MRS. WATTS): Look, I'm not going to do . . .

LUDIE: We're going to stop this wrangling once and for all. You've given me your word and I expect you to keep your word. We have to live together. Live together in peace.

(JESSIE MAE *hands the check back to* MRS. WATTS.)

JESSIE MAE: Go ahead, you keep the check. Don't lose it before you . . . get home. Come on. Let's go. (*Leaves.*)

LUDIE: Mama, if I get that raise you won't have to . . .

MRS. WATTS: Oh, it's all right, Son, I've had my trip. You go on, I'll be there in a minute.

LUDIE (*taking a last look at the house*): This house used to look so big.

(LUDIE *walks away to join* JESSIE MAE. *They continue walking toward the car.* MRS. WATTS *sits down in the grass; she feels the dirt with her hands. After a moment she gets up and starts for the car.*)

MRS. WATTS: Goodbye, Bountiful . . . goodbye.

(*The house is in the background as* MRS. WATTS *walks to the car.* LUDIE *helps* MRS. WATTS *into the backseat, then gets in, starts the car, and begins to drive off.*)

*INTERIOR: BACKSEAT OF CAR.*

MRS. WATTS *looks straight ahead as the car moves back through the fields.*

WOMAN (*voice over, singing*):
>Softly and tenderly Jesus is calling,
>Calling for you and for me.
>See, on the portals he's waiting and watching,
>Watching for you and for me.
>Come home, come home,
>Ye who are weary, come home.
>Earnestly, tenderly, Jesus is calling,
>Calling, O sinner, come home.

*EXTERIOR: COUNTRYSIDE.*

*The car moves through the fields toward the road and slowly disappears.*

*FADE OUT.*